HITLER'S OLYMPICS

Huge crowds gather in a flag-decked Hauptstrasse. (*Author's collection*)

HITLER'S OLYMPICS

The Story of the 1936 Nazi Games

Anton Rippon

Pen & Sword
MILITARY

First published in Great Britain in 2006
and reprinted in this format in 2012 by
Pen & Sword Military
an imprint of
Pen & Sword Books Ltd
47 Church Street
Barnsley
South Yorkshire
S70 2AS

ISBN 1-84884-868-4
ISBN 978-1-84884-868-9

A CIP catalogue record for this book is available from the British Library

Typeset in 11/13pt Palatino by
Concept, Huddersfield

Printed and bound in England by
CPI Group (UK) Ltd, Croydon, CR0 4YY

Pen & Sword Books Ltd incorporates the Imprints of Pen & Sword Aviation, Pen & Sword Maritime, Pen & Sword Military, Wharncliffe Local History, Pen and Sword Select, Pen and Sword Military Classics and Leo Cooper.

For a complete list of Pen & Sword titles please contact
PEN & SWORD BOOKS LIMITED
47 Church Street, Barnsley, South Yorkshire, S70 2AS, England
E-mail: enquiries@pen-and-sword.co.uk
Website: www.pen-and-sword.co.uk

CONTENTS

INTRODUCTION

When the International Olympic Committee met in Barcelona in April 1931 and recommended Berlin as the stage for the 1936 Olympic Games, they awarded them to a democracy. By the time those Games got under way five years later, Germany was in the grasp of a fascist dictatorship and the Olympics had been delivered into the hands of one of the most evil regimes the world has ever seen.

With the benefit of seventy years' hindsight, it is clear that the Nazis achieved a remarkable propaganda coup in 1936. They persuaded the International Olympic Committee and several governments – albeit fairly apathetic ones – that they could stage a fair and free Olympics. And having been allowed to keep the Games, they indulged in a few cosmetic measures – removing anti-Jewish posters for a couple of weeks; ordering their followers to be pleasant to foreigners even if they looked like Jews – which sent most people away with a fairly relaxed view of life in the Third Reich. Visitors went home blissfully unaware that a few miles from the Olympic Stadium a new concentration camp had just been opened. While spectators enjoyed the great athletic spectacle, just a short train ride away, Jews, gypsies, Communists and other enemies of the Nazi state languished with no hope and no future.

Even though Adolf Hitler would surely have proceeded along his chosen road regardless, there is little doubt that staging the 1936 Olympic Games was an important episode in his march which ultimately led the world to another great war.

What follows is an account of the Berlin Olympics: the battles that were fought to prevent them; the extreme measures that were taken to ensure that they went ahead. There are, of course, also the stories of some heroic athletic performances along the way.

But whatever the verdict of history on the IOC's decision made that spring day in Catalonia, one thing is irrefutable: the nature of international sport would be forever changed after 1936; never again would it be possible to successfully argue that sport and politics can be separated. Hitler's Olympics saw to that.

Anton Rippon
Derby, 2006

ACKNOWLEDGEMENTS

A list of principal sources can be found at the back of this book; my thanks go to others before me who have chronicled the many varied aspects of the 1936 Olympic Games. Particularly important have been the learned essays that have appeared in the *International Journal for the History of Sport* and the *Journal of Sport History*. Ottavio Castellini, Statistics and Documentation Senior Manager for the International Association of Athletic Federations was always ready to confirm, or otherwise, the myriad of information concerning athletics records and performances. Constantine E. Zervos and Holly Read of the US National Archives, and Joe Milazzo, Librarian at the Government Information and Map Resources, Central University Libraries, Southern Methodist University, have been prompt in responding to queries and the staff at various newspaper libraries have been enormously helpful. The photographs in Chapter 14 are courtesy of The Melvin C. Shaffer Collection, World War II, 1939–1945: Digital Resources from the Library Collections at Southern Methodist University, Government Information Resources, Central University Libraries, Southern Methodist University, Dallas, Texas, USA (http://digitallibrary.smu.edu/cul/gir/ww2/).

Chapter One

THE MOST EVIL PLACE

On the damp and breezy Saturday of 23 May 1931, Jesse Owens, a 17-year-old African-American student from East Technical High School in Cleveland, arrived at Ohio State University's athletic field in Columbus to compete in his first state scholastic track and field meeting. That afternoon, Owens, the second youngest of eleven children of an Alabama sharecropper, set a new scholastic long jump record, finished second in the 200 yds, and fourth in the 100 yds; it was a modest start but eventually they would name the stadium after him. Ten days earlier, the International Olympic Committee had confirmed that the 1936 Summer Games would be staged in Berlin. Later in 1931, Adolf Hitler would challenge Paul von Hindenburg for the presidency of Germany. The ingredients for a sporting event of legendary proportions were shifting into place.

When, on 13 May 1931, the IOC's recommendation was confirmed by forty-three votes to sixteen – nineteen nations voted at the meeting, forty by postal ballot, with eight abstentions – to choose Berlin ahead of Barcelona, the Weimar Republic, born out of the chaos of Germany's defeat in the First World War, was still the country's democratic government; albeit a fragile one beset by seemingly insurmountable problems of hyperinflation, business failures, crippling reparations and the growth of extreme parties. Two years after the IOC had welcomed Germany back from international isolation – from the end of the war until 1928 they had been banned from even participating in the Olympics – one of those extreme parties engineered a major political change there. On 30 January 1933, in an attempt to stave off a political crisis, President von Hindenburg appointed Hitler, leader of the National Socialist German Workers' Party, as the country's new Chancellor. The Germany that won the Olympic Games was not going to be the same Germany that would eventually stage them.

The conditions that were absolutely perfect for the rise of a man such as Adolf Hitler have been documented perhaps a million times. The Treaty of Versailles, drawn up by the victorious Allies in June 1919, had dismantled the vanquished German empire of Kaiser Wilhelm II. The geography of Europe was redrawn as

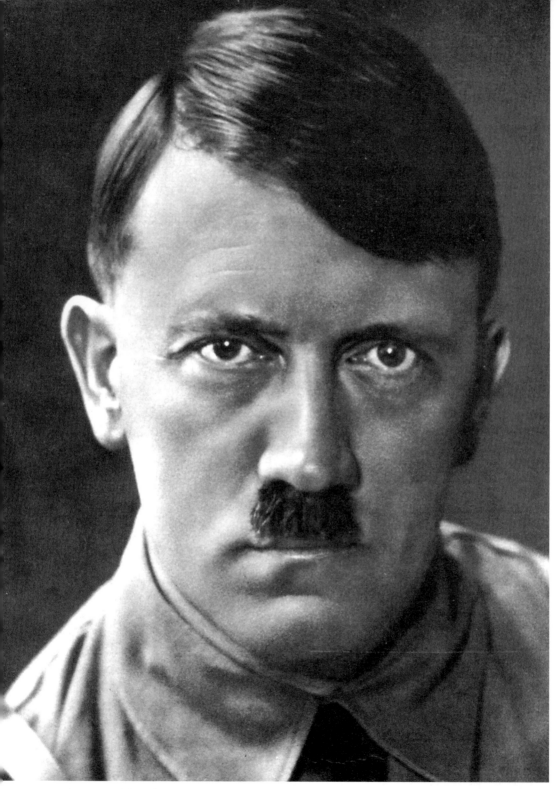

Adolf Hitler in a suitably dynamic pose for the man who saw himself as Germany's saviour. Millions of Germans agreed with him. (*Illustrated London News*)

Germany was made to suffer large territorial losses. In all it lost one million square miles of land – 28,000 of them in Europe – and six million subjects. The Treaty blamed Germany for the war and dictated that reparations, eventually set at £6,600 million, would be paid in monthly instalments. In addition the Germans had to rebuild their economy but the loss of their colonies, and land ceded to other countries, deprived them of rich sources of raw materials. The political impact in Germany itself was enormous. The government of the day refused to sign the Treaty and resigned. The incoming administration had no choice but to agree. And as the economy collapsed – and many old soldiers wondered how Germany could have lost the war when they had still held French territory taken at the very outset in 1914 – the argument that it was the politicians, not the military, who had been responsible for national humiliation gained huge support.

Children use worthless currency as building blocks. By November 1923, 4 trillion German marks would buy just one US dollar, while bank interest rate stood at 900 per cent. (*Illustrated London News*)

Soon, millions distrusted the Weimar Republic in all its manifestations. Even after it had been awarded the Olympic Games, Germany was still the outcast in wider world affairs. Germans were desperate for a strong leader; Hitler's time was drawing near.

Adolf Hitler, third son of a local customs inspector, was born on 20 April 1889 in Braunau-am-Inn, a town on the border between the Austro-Hungarian empire and the German empire. When he was 14, his father died. Five years later his mother also passed away and Hitler moved to Vienna, where he made two failed attempts to enter the Academy for Art, instead being forced to move from one mundane job to another: copying and peddling picture postcards, producing advertisements and painting and decorating houses. In 1913 he moved again, to Munich, where he joined the Bavarian Army. Wounded in the leg and temporarily blinded during the First World War, in which he was awarded the Iron Cross, in 1919 Hitler joined the fascist German Workers' Party whose ideals fitted perfectly with the racism he had first digested as a disaffected youth in Vienna. He climbed swiftly up the party ladder and by 1921 was leader of what had now become the National Socialist German Workers' Party – the *Nationalsozialistische Deutsche Arbeiterpartei* or NSDAP, the Nazi Party. Two years later, the Nazis attempted an armed coup in Munich; when it collapsed, Hitler was imprisoned for nine months in Landsberg prison. Upon his release, instead of the bullet, he determined, for the time being at least, to use the democratic process to gain power.

Despite his comical appearance – a lock of hair falling over his forehead, a square little moustache seemingly capable of independent movement on his pallid, sombre face, often sweating – Hitler proved a mesmeric, rabble-rousing speaker. His targets were manifold: Jews, capitalists, democrats, Communists. The German people were looking for someone – anyone – to blame. Hitler provided them with plenty of targets and they were drawn to him. As well as workers, the Nazis recruited doctors, lawyers, teachers, scientists and members of the upper class. The movement utilized crude symbols of power. Hitler's early followers were called *Sturm Abteilung* or Storm Section – popularly, 'stormtroopers' – who wore a uniform of ski caps, brown shirts, knee breeches and combat boots. Members of the SA also wore swastika armbands, for Hitler had created a Nazi flag, a red banner with a swastika – a hitherto spiritual symbol – on a white circle. Stormtroopers disrupted the meetings of political opponents, and physically attacked people whose race, religion or political persuasion appeared on Hitler's growing list of perceived enemies of Germany. At militaristic rallies they saluted their leader with cries of 'Heil Hitler!'

By 1932, the Nazi Party could no longer be ignored by Germany's political elite; in January the following year, although the Nazis had no overall majority, Hitler was appointed Chancellor of a coalition government. Thereafter he was unstoppable. The ninth and last German federal election of the Weimar Republic was held on 5 March 1933. It was also the last free election to be held in Germany until after the Second World War. Although the Nazis had polled a far greater share of the vote – 43.9 per cent – Hitler was initially forced to maintain his coalition with the Nationalist DNVP. He needed a two-thirds majority to pass the Enabling Act which would allow him to make laws without consulting the Reichstag, the German parliament. The KPD, the largest Communist Party outside the Soviet Union, was already banned, and when the Catholic Centre Party voted with the Nazis, the Act was passed on 23 March. Hitler now also outlawed the Social Democratic Party, itself rooted in the workers' movement. Germany was firmly established as a dictatorship. The Third Reich – Hitler viewed the Holy Roman Empire as the First Reich or empire; the 1871 German Empire as the second – was born.

Members of the SDP and the KPD faced a bleak future. The first concentration camp was already open, not yet for the victims of a mass-extermination programme, but for 'enemies of the State'. The camp, at Dachau, near Munich, held political prisoners together with others who had been condemned in a court of law. Gradually they would be joined by Jews, gypsies, Jehovah's Witnesses, dissenting clergy, homosexuals and just about anyone unwise enough to criticize the Nazis publicly. People were held under *Schutzhaft*, the power to imprison, on the theory of 'protective custody', without judicial proceedings. It was based on a law of 28 February 1933 – the day after the German parliament building had been burned down (by Communists or by the Nazis themselves no one can be sure) – which suspended clauses of the Weimar constitution guaranteeing civil liberties to the German people.

SA guards escort prisoners on fatigue duties at Oranienburg camp in April 1933. (*USHMM, courtesy of National Archives and Records Administration, College Park*)

Initially set up by local SA on an ad hoc basis, camps soon existed throughout Germany. One of the most infamous was Columbia-Haus, a former military prison near Tempelhof airport in Berlin. By mid-1933, the Nazis' secret state police, the Gestapo, was using Columbia-Haus to hold prisoners undergoing interrogation and torture. In late 1935, the Gestapo increased the size of the cells at its headquarters and around the same time, the SS (*Schutzstaffel*; the elite Nazi guard) closed the SA concentration camps it had used to persecute its enemies during the first few years of Nazi power and in their place began building larger camps. Of the original camps, only Dachau survived. Columbia-Haus was shut down on 5 November 1935. A few miles away, work was under way to put the final touches to the Olympic Stadium.

No matter who had been unfortunate enough to be dragged through the gates in the early days of the concentration camps, Hitler's main target would always be the Jews. It seems he felt that their destruction was the very reason for his existence. During his nine months in Landsberg, Hitler, with the help of his secretary, Rudolf Hess, had written *Mein Kampf*, a turgid autobiographical exposition of his political theories, ideas that would later culminate in the Second World War. Prominent throughout this rambling work is the violent anti-Semitism of Hitler and his acolytes. There was a 'Jewish peril', a Jewish conspiracy to gain world leadership. The international language, Esperanto, was part of that Jewish plot. There were also many arguments in favour of the old German nationalist idea of *Drang nach Osten* (drive towards the east): the necessity to gain *Lebensraum* (living space) eastwards, especially in Russia. But always there were the Jews to blame. In his position of dictator, Hitler could at last attend to the menace and, as April 1933 dawned, he began with a boycott of Jewish businesses.

Although this itself was a failure, it marked the beginning of a tragic downward spiral for the Jews, for Hitler had no shortage of supporters for his overall aims. Following its successes of March that year, the Nazi Party had been flooded with applications for membership from people cynically dubbed by the old hierarchy as 'March Violets', latecomers who now jumped on the Nazi train as it gathered steam. The Nazi *Gleichschaltung* – the process by which all existing organizations and associations were nazified, or suppressed – was fully under way. Under the absolute leadership of Adolf Hitler, the state, not the individual, was supreme. From the moment of birth, one existed only to serve the state and obey the Führer.

Millions readily agreed. Bureaucrats, industrialists, even intellectual and literary figures, were attracted by Hitler's crude pageantry. Some of those who disagreed, many of whom had Jewish blood, wisely departed. More than 2,000 of Germany's finest minds, including scientists, engineers, architects, writers, artists and film-makers, fled the country. They included the psychologist Sigmund Freud, the Nobel Prize-winning writer Thomas Mann, film director Fritz Lang, actress Marlene Dietrich, composer Kurt Weill, conductor Otto Klemperer, the great tenor Richard Tauber and the eminent architect Walter Gropius. Ernst Jokl, founding president of the World Physical Exercise Council, also fled. Albert Einstein, widely regarded as the greatest scientist of the twentieth century, was visiting California when Hitler came to power; he never returned to Germany. For those who remained there was now the heady cocktail of fear and optimism, fuelled by a never-ending stream of Nazi parades and rallies. And everywhere there were the flags, thousands upon thousands of them, red, white and black swastika flags and banners. They flew from every flagpole, hung from almost every window, lined every main street.

The boycott of Jewish businesses began at 10 a.m. on Saturday, 1 April 1933. Stormtroopers stood at the doorways to Jewish stores, shops and offices, holding posters proclaiming: 'Germans, defend yourselves against the Jewish atrocity propaganda, buy only at German shops', and 'The Jews are our misfortune'. Most Germans were interested only in a bargain, or in getting their weekend shopping done as quickly as possible, so they ignored the SA and their posters. Saturday was also the Jewish Sabbath and so most of the smaller neighbourhood shops owned by observant Jews were already closed; the brown-shirted stormtroopers found themselves picketing shops that were not even open. There was some violence, however, and in Kiel a Jewish lawyer was killed.

The boycott lasted one day, but it was immediately followed by a series of laws which were much more effective in robbing Jewish people of their rights:

- On the same day as the boycott of Jewish businesses, a law was introduced which banned Jews from teaching in state schools.
- On 7 April, the Law for the Restoration of a Professional Civil Service was introduced, Article 3 of which specified that 'Civil servants who are not of Aryan descent are to be retired; if they are honorary officials, they are to be dismissed from their official status.'

Nazi Brownshirts, with the help of a civilian party member, pasting anti-Semitic posters on Jewish shops. (*NARA 242-H-739*)

- On 11 April came the first legal definition of who was a Jew since the passing of the Enabling Act had given Hitler absolute power: 'A person is to be considered non-Aryan if he is descended from non-Aryan, and especially from Jewish parents or grandparents. It is sufficient if one parent or grandparent is non-Aryan. This is to be assumed in particular where one parent or grandparent was of the Jewish religion.'
- On 22 April, Jews were prohibited from serving as patent lawyers and from serving as doctors in state-run insurance institutions.
- On 25 April, a law against the overcrowding of German schools restricted the proportion of Jews admitted to public education institutions to their proportion in the population.
- On 6 May, the Civil Service law was amended to close loopholes in order to keep out honorary university professors, lecturers and notaries.

- On 2 June, a law was introduced that prohibited Jewish dentists and dental technicians from working with state-run insurance institutions.
- On 14 July, the Nazi Party was declared the only party in Germany, while a law was introduced which allowed for past naturalization to be revoked and German citizenship cancelled. It was primarily aimed at Jews naturalized since 1918 from the formerly eastern German territories.
- On 22 September, the Nazis established the Reich Chamber of Culture; a week later Jews were excluded from all cultural and entertainment activities including literature, art, film and theatre.
- On 28 September, all non-Aryans and their spouses were prohibited from government employment.
- On 4 October, a law was introduced to restrain the free expression of opinion unacceptable or in opposition to the Nazi Party. Jews were prohibited from working as journalists and all newspapers were effectively placed under Nazi control. In addition, anti-Jewish signs were posted throughout Germany, 'Jews not welcome', being one of the milder ones.
- On 10 May 1933 there occurred something as sinister as any of the above. Students from universities hitherto regarded as among the finest in the world gathered in Berlin and other German cities to burn books with 'un-German' ideas. The works of Freud, Einstein and Mann, among many others, went up in flames as students gave the Nazi salute. In Berlin, the Propaganda Minister, Joseph Goebbels, told the book burners: 'The era of extreme Jewish intellectualism is now at an end.'

Within a few months of the Nazis taking control of Germany, millions of its citizens had been condemned to a life of terror. By the end of 1933, it has been estimated, a total of 150,000 people languished in concentration camps. Late that year, at Aschaffenburg camp in Bavaria, a group of SS guards killed several Jewish inmates. The guards were arrested, but SS officers insisted that their men were not subject to civilian authority and Heinrich Himmler, Reichsführer of the SS, demanded that no charges be brought against them. It was a decision that set a precedent for mass murder in concentration camps across the Third Reich.

That the rest of the world was ignorant of the Nazi terror is impossible to imagine, for there was plenty of reference material available for those who chose to read it. After escaping from Germany, Gerhart Segar, a former Social Democrat member of the

Reichstag and secretary-general of the German Peace Society, wrote graphically of his imprisonment in the Oranienburg camp, situated in an abandoned brewery twenty-two miles north of Berlin's city centre. Seger's book, *A Nation Terrorized*, was the first published eye-witness account of Hitler's concentration camps. It came out in Europe in 1934, and in the USA the following year, and sold half a million copies. In the book's foreword, Heinrich Mann, elder brother of the exiled Thomas Mann, wrote: 'You have escaped from one of the most evil places in the world.'

If further evidence was needed, it came in *Fatherland*, also published in the USA in 1935. Paul Massing, arrested for being a member of the Communist Party, provided a graphic testimony to the cruelty of the Nazi regime when he wrote his book under the nom-de-plume of Karl Billinger. In Columbia-Haus, Massing suffered terrible beatings at the hands of the SS:

> The two Blackshirts standing behind me seized me and rushed me downstairs to the cellar, where the 'preparatory squad' was already on hand. From a tin pan they lifted wet horsewhips, which cut sharper after being soaked in water.
>
> 'Pants down!'
>
> I stood motionless. In a moment I lay, stripped from the waist down, across a table. Four men held me; three others flogged me. At the first lash I thought I should leap to the ceiling. My whole body contracted convulsively. Against my will I let out a shrill cry. The second stroke, the third, the fourth – not quickly but at measured intervals, spaced so as to keep me from losing consciousness, to make certain that my nerves would register each blow in all its agonizing pain. I was aware of but one racking desire – to be dead, to be dead, to be dead, and have this over, finished, done. My body did not seem to belong to me any more. After ten or twelve lashes I felt the blows only as dull detonations in my head. I no longer had the strength to cry out. The twenty-fifth stroke was followed by a brief pause, during which the men changed places. One of them poured a pitcher of cold water over my head to render me fit for further treatment. Then they started afresh. When it was over they dragged me back to my cell. Closing the door, they said they would be back shortly to return me to the investigation court.

He wrote: 'In Nazi Germany, it has become a crime to believe that all men are equal in the sight of God.'

The Nazis' obsession with racial purity had not stopped at purging Germany of Jewish blood. In April 1933, the Prussian Minister of the Interior, Hermann Göring, ordered local authorities to produce statistics concerning the 'Rhineland Bastards', the offspring of German women and colonial soldiers who served in the French occupation force in Germany in the 1920s. The remit also covered children of German colonialists who married African women and returned with them to Germany after the First World War. It was agreed that the best way to end this 'black curse' was by sterilizing people of mixed race. The gypsy Roma and Sinti people were also targeted for sterilization.

In June that year, the Committee of Experts for Population and Racial Policy was established by the Interior Minister, Wilhelm Frick. Its main aim was to draft a law for 'the prevention of hereditarily diseased progeny' which effectively meant the sterilization of anyone considered to be 'hereditarily ill'. So-called Hereditary Health Courts were set up to rule on individual cases. Where to draw the line, though? Nazi ideas of racial flaws included schizophrenia and manic depression, as well as Huntingdon's chorea, hereditary blindness, hereditary deafness, hereditary epilepsy and chronic alcoholism. In the next ten years around 400,000 Germans were to be sterilized under this law.

By the end of the year, the Nazis had turned their attention to criminals and other members of what could be regarded as the general lower order; here again there was a hereditary twist to their thinking with claims that habitual criminals had inherited this trait from their forebears. The term 'vagrant' was an extremely vague label and seemed to encompass almost anyone who roused Nazi suspicions but who did not readily fall into one of the more clearly defined categories. Although many of those arrested were soon released, others, seen as 'disorderly vagrants', were imprisoned or forced to join labour schemes. The Law against Dangerous Habitual Criminals already allowed for the imprisonment of anyone with two criminal convictions for an unlimited period in protective custody – that term again – and now it was extended to cover 'beggars, vagabonds, pimps, prostitutes and the workshy'.

It was inevitable that the homosexual community would eventually be targeted and in June 1935, the criminal code was amended to include any form of 'criminal indecency' between men, and behaviour likely to offend 'public morality'. Homosexual men now faced up to ten years in prison. The same month, the Nazis took further steps to cleanse the nation with an amendment to the Law for the Prevention of Hereditarily Diseased Progeny:

compulsory abortions could now be carried out on 'hereditarily ill women or women who become pregnant by a hereditarily ill partner' up to six months into their pregnancy. The Law for the Protection of German Blood and German Honour – one of the so-called Nuremburg Laws passed in September 1935 – already prohibited marriages and extra-marital relations between Aryans and non-Aryans; in November 1935, the Ministry of the Interior introduced rules requiring couples to provide 'testimonials of fitness to marry'. The second Nuremburg Law, the Reich Citizenship Law, stripped Jews of their German citizenship and introduced a new distinction between 'Reich citizens' and 'nationals' intended to prevent 'progeny deleterious to German blood'.

Finally, the Nazis turned upon religion. Jehovah's Witnesses would not undertake military service, and since they also believed in the imminent return of a Messiah who, in their eyes, was obviously not Adolf Hitler, they too were marched into the camps. Roman Catholics might have felt themselves safe after Hitler signed a concordat with the Vatican guaranteeing the freedom of the Catholic Church to conduct its own affairs without interference from the state. That the concordat was negotiated by the former German Chancellor, and now Vice Chancellor, Franz von Papen, the son of a wealthy Catholic family, should have been of additional comfort. But Church leaders who opposed Nazism were not safe; within days of the concordat being signed in July 1934, Catholic priests and nuns were being arrested on trumped-up charges throughout Germany. Then, in Olympic Year, Pastor Martin Niemöller of the Confessional Church published a major document opposing the Nazis' religious policies. Niemöller had been an early supporter of Hitler, and in 1933 had described the Nazi programme as a 'renewal movement based on a Christian moral foundation'. The following year he published his autobiography *From U-Boat to Pulpit*, a right-wing nationalist view of the war and its aftermath which was popular with Nazi Party members and sold 90,000 copies in its first few weeks. He seemed to agree with Hitler's views on race and nationhood, but not with his approach to religion. Now the publication of Niemöller's views triggered a purge of the Protestant Church too.

Yet, despite all this, the average German citizen – provided they were of Aryan stock, heterosexual and hardworking – did not seem to mind trading other people's personal freedoms for the economic miracle that was apparently taking place in their country. When Hitler came to power early in 1933, German unemployment stood at just over six million. By the time the world descended on Berlin for the Olympic Games in 1936 that had fallen to two million. But was it an economic miracle?

There were a number of factors responsible for the drop in numbers, not all of them the sign of a burgeoning economy. Jews had lost their citizenship and were therefore not included in the unemployment figures, even though they had also lost their jobs under the Nazis. Women were removed from the statistics. And the threat of a concentration camp place for the 'workshy' presumably encouraged people to take whatever job was going. In March 1935, Hitler announced that he would introduce military conscription; thousands of young men would soon be removed from the unemployment figures when they were drafted into the army. And an army needs weapons, so the increase in munitions workers further reduced the figure.

There were many tangible benefits, however. The Nazis had introduced a public works scheme and thousands more men were

Workers employed in building the autobahns greet Hitler as he arrives to open another section of Germany's new road network. (*Author's collection*)

Hitler meets members of the Voluntary Labour Service, whose members planted forests, repaired river banks and reclaimed wasteland. (*Author's collection*)

A typical piece of staged Nazi propaganda. These 'country cousins' are apparently enjoying their leisure time by taking part in physical exercise in an idyllic rural setting. (*Author's collection*)

made to join the *Reichsarbeitsdienst* (National Labour Service) to build new autobahns, dig irrigation ditches and plant new forests. The autobahn programme, announced in February 1933, was huge. Hitler himself turned over the first spadeful of earth outside Frankfurt in September that year, and under the direction of chief engineer Fritz Todt the fourteen-mile motorway between Frankfurt and Darmstadt was opened on 19 May 1935. The autobahn programme provided immediate work for 100,000 workers and eventually assured wages for some half a million. It certainly impressed Olympic visitors. Hitler also encouraged the mass production of radios, not least as a means of supplying a steady stream of Nazi propaganda to the German people. Youth unemployment was dealt with by the Voluntary Labour Service and the Voluntary Youth Service, whose members also planted forests, repaired river banks and helped reclaim wasteland.

The German Labour Front, meanwhile, looked after the workers' interests – trade unions had been banned – although in return for not being sacked on the spot, workers could leave their job only with permission from the government which alone arranged new jobs. Leisure time was catered for by the *Kraft durch Freude* (Strength through Joy) which provided state-run courses, pastimes, sports and entertainment. Sport, in particular, had an important role to play in the new Nazi Germany.

Chapter Two

PLAYING UNDER THE NAZIS

'German sport has only one task: to strengthen the character of the German people, imbuing it with the fighting spirit and steadfast camaraderie necessary in the struggle for its existence.' So declared Joseph Goebbels, the Nazis' new Minister of Propaganda, on 23 April 1933.

Of course, Goebbels did not mean *all* the German people: three weeks earlier, Jewish boxers and referees had been banned from domestic championship bouts and all contracts involving Jewish promoters declared invalid. Erich Seelig was then the 22-year-old middleweight and light-heavyweight champion of Germany; he was also a Jew. On 26 February 1933, Seelig had won the light-heavyweight title by beating Helmut Hartkopp at the Flora Theatre in Hamburg. A few weeks later, on the eve of a scheduled defence of his middleweight title in Berlin, Seelig was told that if he entered the ring the following day he would be killed. Stripped of his German titles by the Nazis, he fled to France and then to the USA, fought for both the European and world middleweight championships and was eventually elected to the New Jersey Boxing Hall of Fame.

At least Erich Seelig's story has a relatively happy ending. That of another German boxing champion, Johann 'Rukelie' Trollman, ended in tragedy at Neuengamme concentration camp near Hamburg. Trollman was born at Wilsche, Lower Saxony, in December 1907, a member of the Sinti gypsy tribe. After being denied opportunities as an amateur because of his gypsy background, he turned professional in 1929 and soon proved himself a great attraction. Although a successful middleweight, he was also beating some very good light-heavyweights; and he was a charismatic figure, especially popular with

German champion boxer Erich Seelig was forced to flee Nazi Germany after he was told he would be murdered if he defended his title. (*Puglistica.com*)

women spectators. Promoters could not get enough of Johann Trollman and wherever he fought venues soon sold out. In 1932 he was in such demand that he fought nineteen times inside twelve months. Yet as a Sinti, his chances of being allowed to fight for a national title were remote. By the following year, however, such was his popularity with the boxing public that he could be ignored no longer.

Johann 'Rukelie' Trollman, the gypsy boxer whose life ended in a concentration camp near Hamburg. (*Author's collection*)

On 9 June 1933, in Berlin, Trollman faced the Kiel boxer, Adolf Witt, for Erich Seelig's vacant light-heavyweight title. The German boxing authorities were banking on the Aryan Witt to end their problem with Trollman, but the gypsy would not cooperate and, midway through the bout, with Trollman clearly leading on points, Nazi officials at the ringside ordered a 'no decision' result if he should still be ahead at the end. When that was made public at the end of the twelfth round, a near-riot broke out and the boxing officials, fearing for their safety, quickly reversed the decision and declared Trollman the winner. The crowd cheered, and the new champion wept. One week later he received a letter telling him that he had been relieved of the title because of 'poor behaviour' – crying in the ring – and 'bad boxing'. Again there was uproar among true boxing fans and the authorities resolved to deal with the Trollman issue once and for all. The following month, in the same Berlin arena, he was pitted against the German welterweight champion, Gustav Eder, a murderous puncher from Dortmund. Worse, Trollman was ordered to abandon his usual style and instead stand toe-to-toe, trading punches with his opponent. Either that, or have his licence withdrawn.

Such matchmaking was a travesty, and Trollman's comment on it was to climb into the ring on that June evening with his hair bleached blond and his body patted down with flour to assume the caricature of an 'Aryan warrior'. He could probably have outboxed Eder, but chose to obey instructions, taking punch after punch from the sledgehammer fists of his opponent. By the fifth round Trollman had given everything and was carried from the ring, bloodied and most definitely beaten. A broken man, he fought only ten more bouts, losing eight of them and winning only one.

But even that was not the end of Johann Trollman's tragic story. As a gypsy, he chose to undergo sterilization rather than internment, and eked out a living in boxing booths, at one point having to hide in the countryside to avoid arrest. On the outbreak of war, he somehow managed to join the German Army, but in June 1942, while visiting his family in Hanover, he was arrested by the Gestapo and sent to the Neuengamme camp on the River Elbe. Despite being in appalling physical shape, Trollman was forced to take on the guards in a perverse game of 'who can knock the gypsy out?' in the hope of extra food. On the morning of 9 February 1943, he was murdered by his captors. In 2004, almost seventy years after he was denied the German light-heavyweight title by the Nazis, the German Boxing Federation confirmed Johann Trollman as the 1933 champion and awarded the championship belt to his family.

Daniel Prenn, Germany's number one tennis player who was not selected for the Davies Cup team because he was Jewish. (*Author's collection*)

Boxers were just the first of thousands of non-Aryan German sportsmen and women to suffer the consequences of the Nazis' takeover of every walk of life. Twelve days after the German Boxing Association's ban on Jews, Germany's Davis Cup tennis team dropped Dr Daniel Prenn, ranked number one in Germany for four consecutive years from 1929 to 1932, and number six in the world in 1932. Prenn, born in Poland but a naturalized German, had Jewish ancestry and the German Tennis Federation resolved:

> No Jew may be selected for a national team or the Davis Cup; no Jewish or Marxist club or association may be affiliated with the German Tennis Federation; no Jew may hold an official position in the Federation.

Just in case the point had still not been made, the organization added: 'The player Dr Prenn (a Jew) will not be selected for the Davis Cup team in 1933.'

Following Davis Cup triumphs over Britain's top seeds, Fred Perry and Bunny

Austin, and a victory over America's Frank Shields in 1932, Prenn had been labelled 'Europe's number-one man' by the magazine *American Lawn Tennis*. In a strong letter published in *The Times*, Perry and Austin protested about his omission but the international tennis body took no action. Prenn moved to England and became a British subject. He left the amateur ranks and turned professional, but was hardly welcomed with open arms since Germany had become an important stage for the professional game. Meanwhile, the leading figure in German professional tennis, Roman Najuch, resigned as Poland's Davis Cup coach because of 'Poland's anti-German agitation'. Besides weakening the country's tennis prospects by banning Daniel Prenn, the Nazis would one day also deny Germany at least one world-class Olympic performer in high-jumper Gretel Bergmann, who was Jewish. Sport and politics were now clearly interwoven, in Germany at least.

On 25 April 1933, the Reich Sports Office implemented an 'Aryans-only' policy in all German sports organizations, but the order did not apply to Jewish war veterans or their descendants. On 24 May, however, the German Gymnastic Society decreed that Aryan ancestry was absolutely mandatory for membership of the *Turnvereine* (gymnastic associations) that altogether catered for more than 1.5 million members throughout Germany. This was a hugely significant development. The Turner associations were more than just sports clubs. They were directly connected to the movement started in 1811 by a Berlin schoolteacher, Freidrich Ludwig Jahn, the so-called 'father of gymnastics' who is credited with inventing the parallel bars, balance beam, gymnastics rings, vaulting horse and the horizontal bar. But more even than all that, Jahn was also a patriot whose ideal was to teach young gymnasts to regard themselves as members of a movement that would one day free their country, Prussia, from Napoleonic occupation. He popularized the motto *Frisch, Fromm, Fröhlich, Frei* (Fresh, God-fearing, Happy, Free). His mission was to build strength and fellowship among young people of all classes; once Jahn had been accepted as a patriot not an anarchist – he had been arrested in 1819 on suspicion of treason and would have faced the death penalty had he been convicted – the gymnastic clubs that he fostered were seen for what they were and became centres for German nationalism.

In July 1933, *Der Stürmer*, the Jew-baiting newspaper founded by Julius Streicher, the Gauleiter of Franconia who had taken anti-Semitism to new and obscene depths, commented:

In Canstatt, in Württemberg, the Jew Fritz Rosenfelder recently was kicked out of the local gymnastics association. This is such a matter of course that one actually doesn't need to talk about it. Jews are Jews and therefore they simply don't belong to the German Gymnastics Association.

Those few lines hide a greater tragedy. After being expelled from the local club that he had run for years, Rosenfelder had killed himself. In his suicide note, he said that he was

unable to go on living with the knowledge that the movement to which national Germany is looking for salvation considers me a traitor to the Fatherland ... I leave without hate or anger ... and so I have chosen a voluntary death in order to shock my Christian friends into awareness.

Dr Bernhard Rust, a future Nazis Education Minister, ordered that Jews be expelled from youth and welfare organizations.
(*Author's collection*)

There was plenty going on around them to shock Christians and non-Christians alike. On 2 June, Dr Bernhard Rust, the Minister of Science, Art, and Education for Prussia who would, the following year, be appointed the Nazis' Education Minister, had ordered that Jews be expelled from all kinds of youth and welfare organizations and their privileges rescinded. And so it went on: on 22 July, the All-German Chess Convention excluded Jews from its membership; in August, Jews were barred from entering public swimming pools in a growing number of towns and cities all over the Third Reich; on 8 October, non-Aryans were prohibited from being jockeys, amateur or professional.

Jewish athletes, now barred from practically every German sports club, flocked to separate Jewish associations, although their facilities were no match for those of well-funded German clubs. There were three Jewish sport organizations: Maccabi for Zionists, named after one of the great warriors in Jewish history; Schild (shield) for Jewish First World War veterans who had banded together to combat anti-Semitic attacks and to counter accusations that Jews had shown themselves to be cowards during the war; Vintus (*Verband jüdisch neutraler Turn-und Sportvereine*: Association of Jewish Neutral Gymnastics and Sports Clubs), also Zionist but less political and based primarily in North Rhine-Westphalia. In 1933 there were twenty-five Maccabi clubs with about 8,000 members in total, ninety Schild clubs with 7,000 members, and an unknown number of members in eighteen Vintus clubs. Like clubs in the rest of Germany, most of the Jewish clubs were multi-sports organizations, founded as a gymnastics club with other sections added later. Now separated from the rest of German sport, the clubs played in separate Jewish competitions until 1938 when all Jewish sport was forbidden.

In Bavaria, however, Jewish sports were already prohibited in 1933; and in Cologne, the Bar Kochba club folded that year as it was part of the banned *Arbeiter-Turn-und Sportbund* (ATSB or Workers' Gymnastics and Sports Association) which had 1.3 million members. The German Football Association, in particular, was apparently delighted that the Nazis had destroyed its working-class competitor. Earlier, the Bar Kochba of Berlin had hosted a Jewish sports meeting in the Grunewald Stadium, attracting 2,500 Jewish athletes. In 1934, a Jewish championship meeting in the private Berliner SC arena was attended by over 8,000 spectators.

One of the great disadvantages felt by members of the three Jewish sports organizations was the distance they had to travel to compete against each other. Eventually they amalgamated to become the *Reichsausschuss jüdischer Sportverbände* (German Committee of Jewish Sports Clubs). The Schild, representing Jewish veterans (*Sportbund des Reichsbundes jüdischer Frontsoldaten* or RjF), announced: 'Not only is the athletic activity of the Jewish Youth to be supported, but it is also the explicit goal of the RjF to create a German patriotic feeling among the Jewish youths.' They attempted to gain the leadership of Jewish sport's new umbrella organization but, as with all German sports federations, the Nazis were reluctant to favour any of the old organizations, preferring instead to establish new ones. Whoever led it, however, Nazis were happy enough with the Jewish amalgamation: it gave foreigners the impression that Jewish sport was not excluded, just separate.

The Nazis, obsessed with 'purifying' the 'Aryan race', were thus quick to use sport as a major tool in achieving their aims; having taken steps to remove Jews, gypsies, 'Rhineland Bastards' and the like from the sporting life of the nation, they then set about creating the myth of the 'Aryan warrior'. Artists portrayed athletes as heroic figures with beautifully developed bodies, superb muscle tone and the Nazi idea of classic 'Aryan' facial features: blond hair and blue eyes. (If anyone noticed that not one of the Nazi leaders bore the slightest resemblance to this ideal, then they wisely remained silent.) Nazi sport emphasized the strength and health of the entire community over the sporting achievements of any individual athlete.

Hitler told the nation:

> My education is hard. Weakness must be hammered out. In my schools a youth will be raised from whom the world will shrink in fear ... There must be nothing weak or soft about them. The free and noble gaze of the beast of prey must once again flash in their eyes. I want my youth to be strong and beautiful. They must be trained in all manner of physical education. I want an athletic youth. That is first and foremost. In that way we will expunge the thousands of years of human domestication. I have the pure and noble natural material before me out of which I can form something new.

The Nazis' Reich Sports Minister, Hans von Tschammer und Osten, offered his theory of how sport could build character: 'Physical fitness demands hard repetitive daily exertion of the body. The will grows as bodily strength and physical skill increases. A strong will, and a trust in one's own ability to succeed, is the foundation and basis for character education.' He explained how this character building would benefit Germany:

> The healthy, strong, industrious person works and strives for himself, his family, his job and for the greater good of the community. He is a selfless support for his companions who, when called, knows how to come to the defence of his country. He responds to the needs of his community as willingly as to his own, with attention to the abilities, as well as with understanding of the needs, of his national brothers and sisters. His self-confident strength is truly honoured by his fellow citizens.

Physical exercise became supremely important in schools and universities, where, incidentally, the handling of a light rifle was seen as an essential part of the character-building discipline. It was not always a development well received, however. In 1935, the *Kölnische Zeitung*, a newspaper with a long liberal tradition, told its readers that employers in Germany's industrial heartland were finding it difficult to hire suitable recruits from schools and universities because students were spending more time on parade grounds and sports fields than they were in the classroom. Meanwhile, outside the educational establishments, sports, as well as pastimes like hiking and camping, were being used by Nazi youth groups to bring together boys and girls as one single-minded community with clearly defined aims, even if the participants themselves were not always aware of those aims: the boys were being prepared for war; the girls for motherhood in order to propagate the Aryan nation.

Central to all this was the *Hitler-Jugend* – the Hitler Youth – originally founded in 1922 as the *Jungsturm Adolf Hitler*. Based in Munich, that group served as a recruiting ground for the SA before being disbanded following the abortive coup in 1923. In 1926, the year after the Nazi Party was reformed, a new Hitler Youth was started, this time with the express purpose of recruiting directly for the party. By 1930, the Hitler Youth had over 25,000 members with the *Bund Deutscher Mädel* (League of German Girls) for females aged from 14 to 18, and the *Deutsches Jungvolk* for younger boys and girls. By 1933 – with Hitler Youth membership standing at 2.3 million thanks to other youth movements being forcibly merged into it – Baldur von Schirach was appointed Reichsjugendführer (Reich Youth Leader). A former leader of the Nazi students' union, von Schirach began a huge expansion of the Hitler Youth. By the time Olympic flags and banners were being taken down in Berlin in the autumn of 1936, there were more than five million youngsters wearing the paramilitary uniforms of the Hitler Youth; by 1940 the membership would number well over eight million. By then, of course, membership was compulsory.

Physical and military training took precedence over academic work. Members aspired to gain insignia such as the Homeland Sport Administration sleeve band, while the Proficiency Badge (*Leistungs-Kennzeichen*) was the one to which all boys aspired as it was the basis of all their training. This metal badge was considered so important that a cloth one was produced to be worn on sports kit. And, all the while, there was the incessant indoctrination of young minds. The foreword to the *Proficiency Book for German Youth* stated unequivocally:

Physical training is not the private concern of the individual. The National Socialist movement orders every German to place his whole self at its service. Your body belongs to your country, since it is to your country that you owe your existence. You are

Hitler Youth members on a summer camp in 1935. (*Author's collection*)

responsible to your country for your body. Fulfil the demands of this manual, and you will fulfil your duty to the German people.

When, in May 1931, two years before the Nazi Party came to power, the International Olympic Committee awarded the 1936 Games to Germany, Hitler denounced the Olympics as 'an invention of Jews and Freemasons' and an event 'inspired by Judaism which cannot possibly be put on in a Reich ruled by National Socialists'. The rabidly anti-Jewish *Der Stürmer* later denounced the Games as 'an infamous festival dominated by Jews'. In 1934, Bruno Malitz, Sport Leader of the Berlin SA, sent a booklet *Sport in the National Socialist Ideology* to every sports club in Germany, which condemned international sport because 'Frenchmen, Belgians, Pollacks and Jew-Niggers run on German tracks and swim in German pools' and asked whether the nation really wanted the Olympic Games. But he came to the conclusion: 'As a matter of fact we consider them necessary due to international propaganda.' He added, 'The difference with us will be that no private clubs or associations will name the teams in the name of Germany and put Germany to shame. The State will name the teams.'

Chapter Three

POLITICS AND PROPAGANDA

When the first modern Olympic Games were held in Athens in 1896, Germany was among the fourteen countries represented. Twenty years later, the Germans should have staged the sixth Olympiad of modern times, which was awarded to Berlin by the International Olympic Committee during the 1912 Stockholm Games. The Second Reich thoroughly supported the idea of Germany staging the Olympics, and – thanks largely to the lobbying of one man – the government of the day agreed not only to underwrite the costs of putting on the Olympic festival, but also to pay for the selection and training of the German team.

Two senior officials were charged with the responsibility for overseeing Germany's commitment to host the 1916 Games: Dr Theodor Lewald and Carl Diem. Lewald, born in Berlin in 1860, was a lawyer and high-ranking civil servant in the Ministry of the Interior, chairman of the German Olympic Organizing Committee and a leading figure in Germany's participation in the 1908 and 1912 Games. He was a man with strong views, always ready to argue his case; as Commissioner of Exhibitions for the Imperial Reich he had once risked his political career over the issue of art at the German exhibition during the 1904 World Exposition in St Louis. Now Lewald urged that the Reich should also treat the Olympic Games like a world trade exhibition. Whereas in previous Games, German athletes had effectively represented themselves or their clubs, now the country's international reputation was at stake; government subsidies were needed to ensure that Germany competed at the highest level, Lewald argued. He won the day. The best coaches were employed, rigorous selection trials held, and training camps boasting the best facilities were set up.

Carl Diem was a well known figure in German sport. Born at Würzburg in June 1882, in his younger days he was a good athlete who had helped to found the Marcomannia sports club in Berlin, and then the very first association of Berlin sports clubs. Chairman of the *Deutschen Sportbehörde für Athletik* (German Athletic Board), in 1912 he led the German team at the Stockholm Games. In 1913 he was appointed secretary-general of the *Deutschen Reichsausschusses für Leibesübungen* (German Reich Department of Physical Educa-

The architects of Germany's Olympic bid. Theodor Lewald (left) was a career diplomat who insisted that his government must realize that a successful Games would boost German standing in the international community. Carl Diem (right) was one of the most influential figures in the history of German sport. (*Author's collection*)

tion, the umbrella organization for all sports bodies). In the 1920s he was to help found the world's first sports psychology laboratory, in Berlin.

Diem was the ideal person to join Lewald in ensuring that Germany would stage the best possible Olympic Games in August 1916. But by then, of course, the Battle of the Somme was raging, the First World War having put an end to many dreams, not least Olympic ones. When, twenty years later, Germany was given another opportunity to stage an Olympiad, Lewald and Diem were again the men to lead the way.

After the war, Germany, a nation ostracized by the victors of that conflict, was barred from taking part in the Antwerp Games of 1920 and the Paris Games of 1924. Lewald and Diem, meanwhile, had lobbied tirelessly for their country's return to the sporting world family, and when the Germans were finally readmitted, for the 1928 Amsterdam Games, they did extremely well, finishing with ten gold medals, seven silver and fourteen bronze; only the USA, with twenty-two gold, eighteen silver and sixteen bronze, did better. Great Britain finished well down the order, with a total of twenty medals, only three of which were gold. In Los Angeles in 1932, Germany's tally was disappointing, however: only three gold medals against the USA's forty-one; this time Britain managed four. By then, however, Germany knew that it would stage the 1936 Games.

On 26 May 1930, the German Olympic Committee entertained members of the IOC in Berlin to show them around the city and petition them for the right to host the eleventh modern Olympiad. Other candidate cities were Barcelona, Budapest, Buenos Aires, Cologne, Dublin, Frankfurt am Main, Helsinki, Nuremburg and Rome, and although these included three other German cities, the German OC strongly favoured the capital. Their presentation, although extraordinarily modest by the standards of twenty-first-century Olympic bids, was still impressive. They highlighted the fact that Berlin was at the very heart of Europe, and accessible to the rest of the world by air and sea (if one used German ports and then caught a train). Moreover, five and a half million people could reach Berlin in one hour by express train; seven million in two hours; seventeen million in four hours. That was supposing there would be enough trains to carry them, of course, and that Berlin would not sink under their weight if they all managed to arrive together, but the point was well made. And Germany already had a grand Olympic venue: although it would need modernizing, the stadium in the Grunewald, Berlin's city forest, had been sitting there since before the First World War, when it was built to stage the 1916 Games. There were also plans to build further sports facilities around the German capital in time for 1936.

On 25 April 1931, almost a year after they had been shown around Berlin, the IOC gathered in Barcelona to make their final decision. Germany's Olympic officials continued their offensive, making great play of the fact that Germany should have staged the Games twenty years earlier; they desperately wanted to redeem that lost opportunity, and they would have their chance. On 13 May, after the result of the postal ballot had been added to those who had voted in Barcelona, came the announcement that the 1936 Summer Games would be held in Berlin.

Six days later, the official publication of the Reich Department of Physical Education declared:

> We have been entrusted with the only genuine world festival of our age, in fact, the only one since the beginning of time, a celebration which unites all nations and in which the hearts of all civilized peoples beat in harmony. During the Olympic

fortnight, which comes every four years, the interest of the entire world is concentrated upon the results of the Olympic competition, each nation hoping for the success of its own athletes but nevertheless applauding the victor in a true sporting manner regardless of his nationality. There is no other competition between nations in which the laurels of victory are so coveted but in which, on the other hand, the spirit of combat is so honourable and friendly. These Games are the expression of a new outlook and a new youth. The world expects the German nation to organize and present this Festival in an exemplary manner, emphasizing at the same time its moral and artistic aspects. This means that all forces must be exerted, that sacrifices of a physical as well as financial nature must be made, and there is no doubt but that all expectations will be fulfilled for the advancement of the Olympic ideals and the honour of Germany.

Theodor Lewald, now a hugely influential figure in the Olympic movement, had been key in turning the decision Germany's way. Since retiring from national government in 1923, when he had reached the position of an under-secretary of state at the Ministry of the Interior, Lewald had focused entirely on his involvement in sport. He was president of the German Sports Federation and, since 1919, of the German Olympic Committee itself. In August 1924 he became a member of the IOC and was ideally placed to lobby fellow members in the German cause. The Games secured, the 73-year-old Lewald, and Diem, now 50, travelled to Los Angeles to study preparations for the 1932 Olympics which were to be held in the first two weeks of August that year. On the eve of the Games, Lewald was one of an impressive list of speakers at the first-ever International Recreation Congress.

The German delegation were on a fact-finding mission, but they themselves now had a question to answer. Only one year after the Olympics had been awarded to Berlin, political events in Germany were taking an alarming turn, one which alerted the IOC to potential difficulties come 1936. They wanted to know: if the Nazis had somehow gained power by then, could the Games be staged without political interference from a regime whose views on race, creed and colour, at least, appeared to be diametrically opposed to Olympic ideals? (There is an argument that the cult of the winner – the survival of the strongest and fastest, and contempt for the weaker loser – is central to both Olympic principles and fascist ideology; others argue the Olympic precept that taking part is more important than winning, a view traced back to a speech by an American bishop, Ethlebert Talbot, at the 1908 London Games.)

Whatever his own view on the matter, a Munich banker, Karl Ritter von Halt, the 41-year-old president of the German Track and Field Federation who had represented Germany in the modern pentathlon and decathlon at the 1912 Games, was asked to canvas Nazi opinion. Ritter von Halt, a party member who had the ear of the Nazi hierarchy, made the enquiry and assured the IOC that Hitler would not interfere with the Games; he would not try to stop Jewish, black and other 'non-Aryan' athletes from competing in Berlin. All this might have been hypothetical, an academic point, on the eve of the Los Angeles Games; six months later it was a reality when Hitler became Chancellor.

On 11 November 1932, the German Olympic Committee had authorized Lewald, as its president, to form the special Organizing Committee allowed for by IOC statute. The committee would include representatives of the Reich Department of Physical Education as well as the city of Berlin and would be responsible to the IOC for the presentation of the Games and the

Karl Ritter von Halt, the banker and former Olympian who was asked by the IOC to canvas opinion on the Nazis' response to inheriting the Olympic Games. (*Author's collection*)

observance of Olympic regulations. Although he was himself a Protestant, Theodor Lewald's paternal grandmother was Jewish; if the Nazis won complete power, then his position would be vulnerable. As an experienced political operator, he could see what was coming and, a few days before Hitler was appointed to lead the coalition government, set up the Organizing Committee as a separate, and essentially private, non-profit-making body. He reasoned that, even if the Nazis took control of the Reichstag and were then able to throw him, Diem and his other associates off government sports bodies, they would presumably allow them to continue to work on the new independently run committee. That showed a remarkable degree of faith on Lewald's part, even though, in 1918, he had seen the existing German legal system respected by the incoming Weimar Government following the fall of the old imperial administration.

It also has to be remembered that no one really knew what would be the Nazis' attitude to sport. After Mussolini's fascist Italy had shown an enormous willingness to support sporting activities as a way of bolstering his country's reputation in international competitions, it was reasonable to assume that the Nazis would follow a similar path and encourage the strongest existing organizations with plenty of state funding and other practical help. In Italy, the general secretary of the National Fascist Party, Augusto Turati, had an impeccable sporting background. An international fencer, he was an IOC member from 1930 to 1931, president of the Italian Lawn Tennis Federation from 1927 to 1928, and of the Italian Athletics Federation from 1929 to 1930, and extraordinary commissioner of the Italian Olympic Committee from 1928 to 1930. As far back as 1928, the Italian newspaper *La Gazzetta* had pointed out that fascist society was 'marching at the vanguard of modern sport'. Four years later, Italy had won twelve gold medals at the Los Angeles Games, to finish second in the medals table, behind the Americans. Even though there was no sportsman in the Turati mould among Nazi ranks, it seemed a suitable model to follow and the *Turnvereine* (gymnastics clubs) movement, in particular, anticipated a strong voice in a Nazi Germany. But the new regime would prove determined to wipe the slate clean, eliminate the old rivalries, and create its own state-run sports administration within the Ministry of the Interior. A dark shadow was about to fall on the preparations for the 1936 Olympic Games.

First, though, on 24 January 1933, Lewald's new Organizing Committee held its first meeting in the council chamber of Berlin's Town Hall. Lewald himself was president, Diem secretary-general. In his opening address, Lewald predicted that 4,000 athletes would be accompanied by 1,000 team leaders and trainers, and he strongly recommended the remodelling of the existing Olympic Stadium in the Grunewald so that its capacity would be increased to between 80,000 and 85,000. He wanted sport and art to have equal prominence, and revealed his plans for an Olympic Hymn for which a famous German composer would write the music, an exhibition of ancient art, an IOC reception in the Pergamon Museum, and an Olympic Festival Play in the stadium.

He estimated that the receipts from ticket sales would amount to three million Reichsmarks, a sum to be augmented considerably through the income from rent, advertisements and special Olympic products. The problem of financing the Games had been largely solved through 'the generous cooperation of the authorities'. The

Reich Minister of Economics, Dr Hjalmar Schacht, had given his consent to a large lottery which would run for three years, the German sporting and gymnastic federations had voluntarily declared their willingness to collect the 'Olympic Penny' contribution from all the spectators at sporting events, and the Reich Post Ministry had promised to issue special Olympic postage stamps which would be sold at a slightly extra cost, the surplus to be contributed to the Olympic fund. It was estimated at the time that a total of one million Reichsmarks would be derived from the sale of Olympic stamps alone. Lewald also expressed the hope of being able to raise a private guarantee fund. On behalf of the government, Ministerial Director Pellengahr had declared that the Ministry of the Interior was heartily in favour of the Olympic Games being held Germany and would do all in its power to support them.

The first meeting had gone well, with aims defined, initial tasks allotted, and everyone satisfied that progress would quickly be made. The Organizing Committee now had three issues to resolve before it reported to the IOC during its annual meeting in Vienna in three months' time: the centres of competition; accommodation for the athletes; the date of the games. Six days after their meeting in Berlin Town Hall, however, Lewald and his colleagues were faced with a major distraction: Adolf Hitler emerged from the presidential office of Paul von Hindenburg as the new Chancellor of Germany. Within a few weeks, Hitler had engineered a complete Nazi takeover of the government. The coalition administration was no more, democracy in Germany was dead and, along with every other facet of German life, the nation's sporting affairs were now in the hands of a dictatorship whose very existence was founded on racial discrimination and religious persecution.

On 16 March, eight weeks after the Organizing Committee's inaugural meeting, Lewald and the committee's vice-chairman, Heinrich Sahm, Berlin's mayor who had been actively collecting signatures for von Hindenburg to stand again for president, were received by the new Chancellor. They explained to him the significance of the Games, the committee's plans for their presentation, and some of the difficulties they faced. The previous year, Hitler had denounced the Olympics as 'an invention of Jews and Freemasons'. Now he apparently viewed them in a different light. According to an official statement published in Germany's national newspapers, the Führer now welcomed the Olympic Games to Berlin and would do everything possible to ensure their successful presentation. The Games, he declared, would contribute substantially towards furthering understanding among the nations of the world and would promote the development of sport among the German youth, this being, in his opinion, of vast importance to the welfare of the nation. Hitler expressed his best wishes to the Organizing Committee for the success of its work and promised it his constant support.

That day, Lewald had also taken the opportunity to talk to the new Propaganda Minister, Joseph Goebbels. The first ministry created in Hitler's Germany had been the *Reichsministerium für Volksaufklarung und Propaganda* (Public Enlightenment and Propaganda, or Promi). Its first minister was the 35-year-old Goebbels, born into a strict Catholic family in Rheydt (now Mönchengladbach). A crippled foot – the result of contracting osteomyelitis (inflammation of the bone marrow) as a child, and a subsequent operation that resulted in one leg being two inches shorter than the other – had rendered him unfit for military service in the First World War. After earning a Ph.D. for literature and philosophy from Heidelberg University in 1921, he had worked as a journalist; in 1926 he had a novel, *Michael*, published. Like almost all the Nazi leadership, Goebbels was as far removed from the Aryan physique as it is possible to imagine: small of frame, dark of mane, and, of course, in his case, crippled. But he was a powerful man in other ways. As Hitler's Propaganda Minister, Goebbels enjoyed complete control over radio, press, cinema and theatre. Although initially preoccupied with the many other aspects of his ministry, he would soon come to appreciate the importance of the Olympic Games as a weapon in his armoury. Unlike Mussolini, who appears to have had a genuine interest in sport, neither Goebbels nor Hitler, nor any other member of the Nazis' most inner circle, cared anything for it. But now both men saw the significance of the Berlin Games. In a second meeting, on 28 March, Lewald and Diem submitted their publicity and transportation plans to Goebbels, who arranged for the setting up of an Olympic Games Propaganda Commission under the chairmanship of William Haegert, a Promi official. It was to hold its first meeting on 15 January 1934; among its members were, yet again, Lewald, Diem and Ritter von Halt, and the high-ranking Brownshirt, Hans von Tschammer und Osten.

While Goebbels had been settling into his new role, von Tschammer und Osten had also been taking stock of his new job. Ten years older than Goebbels, von Tschammer und Osten found himself in overall charge of all German sport as the Nazis' first Reichssportkommisar (later Reichssportführer; Reich Sports Leader), within the Ministry of the Interior. Several leading sports officials were already members of the Nazi Party, and Lewald, with his Jewish ancestry, was facing increasing prejudice from within the Reich Department of Physical Education; on 12 April 1933, he was forced to resign as its president, although allowed to remain as an honorary member. Diem, whose wife's grandmother was also Jewish, lost his post of secretary-general when the department was replaced by von Tschammer und Osten's new department. The Reich Department of Physical Education had its fate sealed by a three-man committee comprising Heinrich Pauli (German Rowing Association), Felix Linnemann (German Football Association) and Edmund Neuendorff (German Gymnastic Society). In May, with no mandate to do so, they recommended the dissolving of the department and the handing over of all of its funds to the Ministry of the Interior's new sporting body. It came as no surprise that the person who interpreted the committee as lawful and competent was none other than von Tschammer und Osten himself,

Hans von Tschammer und Osten, the high-ranking SA officer who became the head of German sport. (*Author's collection*)

the man who also would replace Lewald as president of the German Olympic Committee, although not as president of the Organizing Committee. Hitler was now very keen to stage the Games and if he interfered with the OC and disposed of Lewald, then, as would be made clear at the Vienna meeting that summer, the IOC would be forced to take the Games away from Berlin.

Stepping into his post of Reich Sport Leader on 28 April 1933, von Tschammer und Osten created around a dozen specialized departments to cover major sports. Henceforward, only these departments would be allowed to organize championship competitions. For instance, the story of the German FA Cup began with the Nazis and, until the end of the Second World War, the trophy bore the Reich Sport Leader's name and was known as the *Tschammerpokal*; the *Deutscher Fussball Bund* (German Football Association, or DFB) simply went along with all this. Guido von Mengden, the DFB's press officer who became one of the most influential men in German sport, wrote: 'National Socialism has restored the meaning of sport.' He was so convinced, he even added: 'Footballers are the political soldiers of the Führer.'

On the face of it, von Tschammer und Osten seemed a clubbable man, happy to play the raconteur as he drank fine wine and viewed the ladies with a roving eye. This jolly demeanour hid a dark side. A veteran of the First World War, von Tschammer und Osten had joined the Nazi Party in 1929; three years later, he was leading member of the SA, a man who enjoyed strutting around in its military uniform. His local branch alone had been responsible for the murder of many Germans, sportsmen and sportswomen among them. Helmut Schön, who would manage West Germany to World Cup soccer glory in 1974, remembered von Tschammer und Osten as a good-looking but 'conceited and pompous man'. Handsome or otherwise, he was now the new face of German sport.

It was a perverse affair. As Hans von Tschammer und Osten's department joined enthusiastically in ensuring that Jews, gypsies, citizens of mixed-race and all political opponents of Nazism were denied their sporting opportunities, so Goebbels's ministry set about trying to camouflage the brutal outrages being perpetrated against non-Aryans, sporting or otherwise. Its efforts met with little success; accounts of what was happening in Germany inevitably reached the attention of the IOC, whose members were, by the very nature of the organization, scattered throughout the world; Hitler's opinions on Jews had also been trumpeted abroad. The Games might still be three years away; the Nazis may have been in absolute power for only three months. But the Americans, in particular, wanted guarantees. Perhaps by making a stand now, the Olympic movement could play its part in halting the abuses already being carried out in the name of the Third Reich. At the very least it might put the Nazis on their best behaviour for a while. At private functions before the IOC's annual meeting, held at the Festive Hall in Vienna's Academy of Sciences on 7 June 1933, the American delegation let it be known that, if the Nazi position remained unchanged, they doubted very much whether the Games could go ahead in Berlin. The German delegation began to make telephone calls.

The morning of the first session passed with the usual welcoming speeches. Then, after lunch, the IOC president, Count Henri de Baillet-Latour of Belgium, apprised his colleagues of the negotiations which had taken place with the German representatives in order to be quite sure that the guarantees given by the government in power in 1931, just as they had been given by the governments of countries where preceding Olympiads had been organized, could be considered as reliable, and that the application of the Olympic rules dealing with the Committee of Organization and the qualifications of participants would be scrupulously observed, even though certain limitations of our International Rules should seem to be inconsistent with recent orders laid down in Germany.

The official report of the annual meeting continues:

The President paid tribute to the Olympic spirit and to the loyalty of the German delegates, who, having done all they could to put the suitable ministers in possession of the facts of the situation, had succeeded in putting matters sufficiently in order in time to allow the following statement to be published today:

The President of the International Olympic Committee asked the German delegates if they would guarantee the observance of the articles in the Charter dealing with the Organizing Committee and the Rules of Qualification.

On behalf of the three delegates, His Excellency, Dr Lewald, replied that, with the consent of his Government:

1. The German Olympic Committee has delegated the mandate, which had been entrusted to it, to a special Organizing Committee as follows: Dr Lewald (President); Duke of Mecklenburg-Schwerin [a horse breeder and former royal governor to Togo]; Dr Ritter von Halt; Herr Von Tschammer (President of the German Olympic Committee); Herr Sahm (Mayor of Berlin); Herr Diem (Secretary of the German Olympic Committee).
2. All the laws regulating the Olympic Games shall be observed.
3. As a principle German Jews shall not be excluded from German teams at the Games of the eleventh Olympiad.

After Lewald's declaration, William May Garland, one of the US delegates and a man who had played a key role in Los Angeles's staging of the 1932 Games,

wished to have it known that the American Olympic Committee, who were desirous of having the United States strongly represented at the next Olympic Games in Europe, would have had to give up participation altogether if German Jew athletes had not been assured the same terms as members of the same faith in other countries.

Another US delegate, Brigadier General Charles Hitchcock Sherrill, a diplomat and former Ivy League sprinter, added that 'the satisfactory statement made by the president would give great pleasure in the United States'.

The response which Lewald had been authorized to make was the one that IOC members wanted to hear. Their first question – whether the Organizing Committee would continue to be selected in accordance with Olympic regulations – had stemmed from the fact that some Nazis were still calling for Lewald and Diem, with their Jewish connections, however tenuous, to be removed. Indeed, in the months prior to the National Socialists coming into power, Diem had fallen foul of Nazi students at his Berlin university, and only a month before the IOC meeting in Vienna, both he and his wife had been dismissed from their posts there.

It should be noted that the German Organizing Committee's executive also included State Secretary Hans Pfundtner, Reich and Prussian Ministry of the Interior; Lieutenant General Walter von Reichenau, Commanding General of the Seventh Army Corps; Major General Ernst Busch, Commander of the 23rd Division; Count Helldorff, Chief of the Berlin Police; Dr Julius Lippert, State Commissioner; Dr Leonrado Conti, Councillor in the Reich and Prussian Ministry of the Interior; State Secretary Walter Funk, of Promi; and Paul Hamel, who was appointed treasurer. In addition, thirty-two other members represented various government ministries including the military, sports bodies, the media and transport organizations. The IOC, however, were most concerned about Lewald and Diem. There was no doubt that the host state had to become involved in organizing the Olympics, but not to the point where its own political appointees were running them. Hitler now had to keep Lewald and Diem, or lose the Games. The IOC's other point was the selection of the German team. Lewald had guaranteed that Jewish competitors would not be excluded as a matter of principle. That left an awful lot of latitude for those responsible for the selection process.

None the less, the immediate threat to Berlin's staging of the Summer Games was removed by this guarantee from such a distinguished Olympic figure as Theodor Lewald. Further, the Winter Games could now be confirmed as Germany's. They would take place from 2 to 16 February 1936 in Garmisch-Partenkirchen (the Bavarian towns were then separate, merging in 1935 in anticipation of the Winter Olympics). Lewald also announced that the president of the Winter Games Organizing Committee would be Karl Ritter von Halt. The German delegates left Vienna feeling that they had achieved what had been expected of them. There were, however, many more political hurdles to overcome.

Chapter Four

THE BOYCOTT THREAT

Five days before Theodor Lewald felt able to assure the IOC that no Jewish athletes would be barred from the 1936 Olympic Games in Germany, all Jews in that country had been expelled from youth and welfare organizations. Indeed, the very same day as Dr Rust's announcement on that matter, Lewald's own position on the Organizing Committee had, itself, still been in doubt. Then Jewish jockeys were banned from their sport. Jews were kicked out of the national chess championships. Jews were prevented from using public swimming pools. And, near Stuttgart, Fritz Rosenfelder killed himself because he could not face expulsion from his gymnastics club just for being a Jew. Clearly, despite encouraging noises made by the German delegates in Vienna, there was still much to concern the IOC in the coming months.

One man seemed convinced, though. Brigadier General Charles Sherrill, a New York Republican who had been the US minister in Argentina and its ambassador to Turkey, is the man credited with inventing the sprinters' crouch start when he was running for Yale in the late 1880s. He was also a US delegate at the Vienna meeting and was not slow in taking most of the credit for wringing out of the Nazis the promise that Jews could compete in Berlin. Three months before Vienna, the American Jewish Congress had organized a mass meeting in New York City's Madison Square Garden, where the Hungarian-born Rabbi Stephen Wise, one of the most powerful and respected leaders of America's Jewish community, had called for an immediate end to the anti-Semitism of the Third Reich. Sherrill had sent a telegram: 'Rest assured that I will stoutly maintain the American principle that all citizens are equal under all laws.' Now Sherrill wrote to Wise again, highlighting his own involvement in the IOC's apparent triumph.

He concluded:

It was a trying fight. We were six on the executive committee, and even my English colleagues thought we ought not to interfere in the internal arrangements of the German team ... The Germans yielded slowly, very slowly. First they conceded that the other nations could bring Jews. Then, after the fight was over, telephones [calls] came from Berlin that no publication should be given to their government's back-down on Jews, but only the vague statement that they agreed to follow our rules ... Then I went at them hard, insisting that as they had expressly excluded Jews, now they must expressly declare that Jews would not even be excluded from German teams. All sorts of influence was exerted to change my American stand. Finally they yielded because they found that I had lined up the necessary votes.

Theodor Lewald, meanwhile, had been relegated to the role of the respectable face of Germany's Olympic dream. He must surely have known that what he was saying carried no weight, that he was simply being used to allay the fears of foreign governments. Yet he appears to have mistakenly felt that he could continue to serve the best interests of sport, even under a fascist regime; that is, if one accepts that such a public figure even had the opportunity to say 'no' to the Nazis. What is certain is that, whatever Lewald had promised in Vienna, in the weeks and months that followed, an increasing number of developments laid bare the Hitler regime's real attitude to sport. Despite Charles Sherrill's triumphant letter to Rabbi Wise, it was clear to many people in America that Nazi Germany was probably the last place on earth that should be holding an Olympic Games.

Avery Brundage, president of the American Olympic Committee. Brundage coveted a place on the IOC and was desperate for the boycott issue to be resolved peacefully. (*Author's collection*)

As early as April 1933, the *Baltimore Jewish Times* had asked Avery Brundage, president of the Amateur Athletic Union (AAU) and of the American Olympic Committee, for a reaction to the Nazi boycott of Jewish shops and the general plight of Jews in Germany following Hitler's rise to power. The next day, the *New York Times* ran the headline: '1936 Olympic Games May Be Cancelled Due To Germany's Campaign Against Jews'. Brundage, who had studied civil engineering at the University of Illinois and founded a building company in his native Chicago, had been a good all-round athlete himself. He had competed in the pentathlon and decathlon events at the 1912 Stockholm Games (as had Karl Ritter von Halt, now a German IOC representative and Nazi Party member) and had also won the US national all-round title on three occasions. In 1930, he had added the vice-presidency of the International Amateur Athletic Federation (IAAF) to his list of sporting offices.

Brundage told a newspaper reporter:

My personal, but unofficial, opinion is that the Games will not be held in any country where there will be interference with the fundamental Olympic theory of equality of all races. The Olympic protocol proves there shall be no restriction of competition because of class, colour, or creed.

Otherwise he felt that the Games might be transferred to one of the other bidding cities – Tokyo, Barcelona, Rome perhaps – or they could be cancelled altogether, as they were in 1916, ironically the only other time that Berlin had been scheduled to stage them. And, of course, if they went ahead and were boycotted by enough countries, then Germany would lose out anyway, since that would be a massive propaganda own-goal. In the end, though, said Brundage, he fully expected the issue to be resolved when the IOC convened in Vienna in June. A day after the New York Times headline suggesting that the Berlin Games might be cancelled, the newspaper ran an interview with Lewald's Olympic partner, Carl Diem, who professed shock that the Games might be in jeopardy, adding that there was no discrimination in German sport.

On the first day of the Vienna meeting – to underline that, whatever was being claimed by the German delegates, the facts were rather different – the New York Times also reported a statement by Edmund Neuendorff, head of German gymnastics:

Misunderstandings have arisen out of my recent decision in 'Aryanizing' the Turner [gymnastics] organisations that an exception should be made of Jews who have fought at the front, sons and daughters of Jews who fell in battle, and fathers and mothers of sons who died. I therefore cancel the above exceptions and hereby decree that all male and female Turner of Jewish descent as far back as grandparents must be separated from our organization.

That, if nothing else, would have told the IOC that there was trouble ahead, whatever Lewald was telling them. It was certainly a sea change from the situation of October 1932, when Rabbi Wise had received a report from a scholar whom he had sent to Germany and who had interviewed thirty leading Jews, all of whom except one had declared that 'Hitler would never come to power'.

Throughout the summer of 1933, American Jewish and anti-Nazi organizations lobbied for the United States to help Germany's half a million Jews, beleaguered in a population of 67 million. The question of the USA's participation in the Berlin Olympics was never far from the top of their agenda. The Americans traditionally sent the biggest teams to the Olympics, and won the most medals. Their reaction, more than anyone else's, was crucial. Nevertheless, no one expected the storm that broke in November, when the Amateur Athletic Union held its annual meeting in Pittsburgh. The AAU passed a resolution that it would not authorize any American athlete to compete in Berlin until the German Olympic Committee had changed its position 'in fact as well as theory' so that German athletes of Jewish heritage or faith were encouraged to 'train, prepare for, and participate in the Olympic Games of 1936'.

The only outright opposition was voiced by Dietrich Wortmann, who had represented the USA as a wrestler at the 1904 Olympics in St Louis and was now the AAU's first weightlifting chairman. Wortmann, from the German-American Sports Club in New York, pointed out that it was all very well the United States insisting that there should be no discrimination against Jewish competitors in Germany. But since the American track and field champion-ships had recently been moved from New Orleans to Lincoln, Nebraska, in order that African-Americans could take part, and since the national boxing championships had been switched from Baltimore to Boston, again to ensure that African-Americans could participate, the AAU had little right to tell other countries how to behave when there was racial discrimination in American sport too. Other critics added weight to that argument, pointing out that all the black athletes likely to make the US team in 1936 would come from the northern colleges that catered for mostly white students; this showed how poor were the facilities at predominantly black colleges. Another dissenting voice, but for a different reason, was that of Bill Henry, a *Los Angeles Times* journalist and member of the American Olympic Committee. He thought that as the IOC was based in Europe, they should make any decisions concerning the Berlin Games. 'This country would be a lot better off,' he wrote: 'if it left the decision regarding the fitness of Germany to hold the Games to the international body.'

Berlin's reaction to the boycott threat was immediate. The German Organizing Committee sent a telegram to the AAU meeting, urging them to accept that, after the IOC meeting in Vienna, they had done everything to honour the promises made there. The telegram was read to AAU delegates, many of whom were also attending the American Olympic Committee conference to be held in Washington immediately afterwards. When the resolution threatening to refuse accreditation to American athletes for the Berlin Games was put to the AOC, Charles Sherrill spoke out against it, eventually succeeding in tempering it down so that it was more 'a protest and not a threat'. It is hard to understand why Sherrill was so convinced that the German pledge would hold good. Perhaps it was for no other reason than he regarded himself as being its main broker. He had set so much personal store by it, how could he now believe that it was worthless? In truth, all he had achieved was to pressure Germany into saying almost anything in order to retain the Games. But while AAU delegates found it hard to accept that conditions in Germany were becoming anything but worse for Jews and other non-Aryans, there were enough AOC members who could be convinced otherwise.

While Sherrill had his reasons for not seeing the dangers looming large in Nazi Germany, another American diplomat was trying desperately hard to alert his masters. Eventually, he would also become deeply involved in the debate over boycotting the 1936 Games. George Strausser Messersmith was born in Fleetwood, Pennsylvania, in 1883. His forebears were Presbyterians from the Rhineland. In 1914, Messersmith left his job as a schoolteacher in Delaware to join the Foreign Service, being based first at Fort Erie in Canada. At his second post, in Curacao in the Netherlands West Indies during the First World War, he had cracked a German code which allowed the US to arrest and deport enemy agents. Messersmith served next in Antwerp, Buenos Aires, and, in 1930, became Consul General in Berlin. He was to be described as 'probably the most fearless and determined foe Hitler's gang faced, then or ever, among Western diplomats'.

On 26 June 1933, three months after the Nazis began their systematic takeover of every aspect of German life, Messersmith wrote to William Phillips, the American Under Secretary of State. Part of his letter read:

> If this Government remains in power for another year and carries on in the same measure in this direction, it will go far towards making Germany a danger to world peace for years to come ... With few exceptions, the men who are running this government are of a mentality that you and I cannot

understand. Some of them are psychopathic cases and would ordinarily be receiving treatment somewhere. Others are exalted and in a frame of mind that knows no reason. The majority are woefully ignorant and unprepared for the tasks which they have to carry through every day.

On 23 November, Messersmith wrote again to Phillips: 'Everything is being done to … stimulate military training and exercises, and innumerable measures are being taken to develop the German people into a hardy, sturdy race which will be able to meet all comers. The military spirit is constantly growing.'

Five days later he wrote yet again, expressing fears that the Nazis might allow a few Jews to train with Olympic hopefuls in order to hide their true intentions:

It should be understood that this will be merely a screen for the real discrimination which is taking place … similar to that which they [the Nazis] took in permitting Dr von Lewald to remain on the Olympic Committee … Personalities such as Dr Lewald … are being used to endeavour to give the outside world improper or incomplete pictures of the situation here. This form of propaganda is a definite and favoured instrument of the Ministry of Propaganda.

Messersmith's fears were soon realized. Just two weeks later, Lewald met with Hitler and suggested that, if a few Jewish athletes were allowed into the training camps to prepare along with other Olympic prospects, then the whole American problem would probably blow over. Lewald followed up with a letter to Hans Pfundtner at the Ministry of the Interior. If the AOC followed the example of the AAU, he told Pfundtner, and pulled out of the 1936 Olympics, then the IOC would almost certainly relocate the Games, probably to Italy or Japan. The next IOC convention, scheduled for Athens in May 1934, was crucial. By then, Germany had to have convinced the Americans.

Two months before the American delegation left for the spiritual home of the Olympic Games, however, an event turned up the temperature still further. In March 1934, the American Jewish Congress and the American Federation of Labor sponsored a mock trial and anti-Nazi protest rally at Madison Square Garden. The German ambassador, Dr Hans Luther, protested, but Cordell Hull, the Secretary of State, pointed out that he had no power to prevent the rally. It was a remarkable event: over 20,000 turned up, to hear some twenty witnesses give evidence against Adolf Hitler and his government. There was one empty chair: Hans Luther did not appear to defend his country. Two leading Democrats, Fiorello LaGuardia, the Italian-Jewish Mayor of New York City, and the liberal Catholic Al Smith, four-times Governor of New York State, both testified as the Nazis were 'tried' for crimes against civilization. Smith said that Hitler had returned Germany to 'the law of the caveman'. (Smith was later to describe 'economics, unchecked and in ignorance of the land and rent question' as 'the caveman's law', so it was a favourite phrase of his.) The same day, in Berlin, the American ambassador, William Dodd, had a long meeting with Hitler. Dodd expressed concern for 'the Jewish situation as existing in New York' and referred to the mock trial of Nazism being held there. Hitler repeatedly interrupted, shouting 'Damn the Jews', and promising that if foreign intervention continued on behalf of the Jews, he would 'make an end of all Jews in Germany'.

Even if the Führer and the American ambassador were speaking behind close doors, such events as the mock trial ensured that the question of the Jews in Germany was always before the American public. As the American delegates prepared for their trip to Greece, newspaper headlines across the country would not let them forget the issue, while columnists asked whether the Games could really be staged in Berlin, pointed out that in Germany Jews had lost their birthright, and wondered if the Nazis really felt that it was only Jews and left-wing activists who were organizing opposition abroad. Did it not perhaps occur to them that practically the whole civilized world was against what they were doing?

Behind the scenes, however, Avery Brundage coveted a place on the IOC and desperately wanted peace to break out. In the autumn of 1933, he had asked the IOC president, Count Baillet-Latour, for advice about how to proceed. He did not, he said: 'want to embarrass the IOC'. The Count told Brundage that he should not always believe everything that was said by 'the other side', adding that while he himself wasn't 'personally fond of Jews and of the Jewish influence', he would not have them 'molested in any way whatsoever'.

In early May 1934, the IOC executive committee met in Brussels on its way to Athens. The official publication lists only the relatively mundane business of the day, including a report from a committee set up to discuss the definition of amateurism. The *New York Times*, however, was able to report that Theodor Lewald had pointed out to his executive colleagues that, of the 412 athletes to have represented

Germany in the 1928 and 1932 Olympics, only three had been Jews; there may not be any Jewish athletes good enough to compete in 1936 anyway. Sherrill put across much the same point: in 1932 there had been only five Jews out of 400 American competitors. Lord Aberdare, one of Britain's delegates, warmed to the theme: only one Jew out of seventy-four of his country's team in Los Angeles. It seems that everyone was trying to persuade everyone else that this question of whether Jews could compete in Berlin was getting out of proportion. Whether Germany, or anyone else, even had any Jewish sportsmen and women of Olympic standard rather missed the point. It was, after all, a moral issue.

The Athens conference was into its third day before the question was raised again. On the morning of 18 May 1934, in the big hall of the National Academy in the Greek capital, after several other items of business, Theodor Lewald rose to give an account of how preparations were progressing for the Berlin Games. He told the conference about proposed alterations for the transformation of the Olympic Stadium: the demolition of the racecourse; the erection of new buildings near the stadium; the Olympic Village; the swimming venue; the rowing course and the organization for the yachting competitions, all of which would take place at Kiel. Then Karl Ritter von Halt gave a detailed report on the Winter Games to be held at Garmisch-Partenkirchen, and the conference heard that the German Organizing Committee was going to issue a magazine, *Olympique*, of which 13,000 copies were being printed, to make their plans known to the whole world. The demonstration of a German sport would be that of gliding, although the foreign demonstration sport had not yet been decided. Lewald then asked the IOC to approve plans for the torch run from Olympia to Berlin, which they did.

Everyone was now waiting for the inevitable question. It came from Lord Aberdare, who told delegates that, owing to 'new and violent opposition in the press and by letter to the holding of the Games of 1936 in Germany, and the fear that during the Games anti-Semitic manifestations might take place', there was now a hesitancy in Britain about taking part in Berlin. Aberdare asked the German representatives whether the pledge made in Vienna the previous year had been given practical application and if it really was possible for Jews to go into training with the object of participating in the Olympic Games. If a declaration on those points could be made, he said, then it would tend to reassure public opinion. William Garland expressed much the same opinion, adding that owing to the 'exaggerated campaign of the American press', fears might be entertained that the necessary votes for US participation at the Games in Berlin might not be obtained.

Baillet-Latour said that he was conscious of the serious efforts his German colleagues had made to keep sports outside politics in their country. He now asked them to make a declaration, based on precise facts 'in order to put a stop to these press campaigns'.

The German delegates responded. First, Karl Ritter von Halt declared emphatically that the pledge given in Vienna had been 'loyally kept'. Every facility was given to non-Aryans to take part in the Games and to train for them. He mentioned the case where Jewish athletes of recognized quality had been invited to participate in Berlin. Besides this, he said, Jewish organizations in Germany had been invited to send in their proposals and had given in the names of numerous athletes for the selecting competitions. Preparation by non-Aryans was possible.

Then it was Theodor Lewald's turn to speak. He would, he said, not only give his assurance that the pledges made in Vienna had been met, but could also state that they had been 'enlarged upon'. He would give precise details of the measures taken which would enable unknown Jewish athletes to come forward. According to Lewald, it would be absolutely impossible for 'manifestations to take place during the Games'. Germany had respected and would respect entirely the pledges given in Vienna.

Baillet-Latour lent his weight to the beleaguered Germans. He was under the impression, he told the conference, that political parties hostile to the Germany of today were seeking to use the Olympics in order to launch their attacks. The political side of the question had nothing to do with the IOC, who took care to see that sports remained outside politics. Personally he considered the assurances given by his German colleagues satisfactory and asked them to give an official declaration on these points.

The official bulletin of the IOC records:

> To meet the wishes of the president and to reply to the questions asked by Lord Aberdare and Mr W M Garland, and desirous of giving precise information to the National Olympic Committees about the pledges given in Vienna in 1933 concerning the admission of Jews and the possibility for preparation for the Games by non-Aryan athletes, S. E. Dr Lewald and Dr Karl Ritter Von Halt made the following declarations:
>   1. It goes without saying that the pledges given by Germany in Vienna in 1933 to admit to the German Olympic

team German sportsmen of non-Aryan origin, provided they have the necessary capability, will be strictly observed and facilities for preparation will be given to all sportsmen.

2. For this purpose the *Leichtathletikverband* (German Amateur Athletic Federation) has invited the *Reichsbund Judischer Frontsoldaten* (Association of Jewish Ex-Servicemen) and the *Makkabikreis* (Maccabi) to notify them of the names of intending competitors for training purposes, and the first of the two above associations had already so promised by a letter of 15 March 1934.

3. With regard to the choice of an 'Unknown Sportsman' it was only necessary that the nationality should be German and all non-Aryan talent would be admitted for training.

4. The fear of manifestations against Jewish sportsmen was absolutely groundless, considering the sportsmanship and discipline of the German people. The German members gave their most emphatic guarantee.

The bulletin then reported:

The Committee, considering that the political side of the question did not come within their competence but that they had the duty of watching to keep sports outside politics, received with satisfaction the above declaration and state that the facts put forward by the Organizing Committee of the eleventh Olympiad prove absolutely that all has been done to put the German athletes in a position of complete equality.

Everyone was happy then? Apparently not. When the American Olympic Committee met two weeks later, there was still strong opposition from some quarters to taking part in the Berlin Olympics. Even von Tschammer und Osten's announcement that twenty-one Jewish athletes, including Germany's women's high-jump champion, Gretel Bergmann, had been invited to special Olympic training camps, did nothing to quieten protests in the USA.

In the mean time, the AOC had decided to send its president Avery Brundage to Germany, to investigate the situation first-hand. It was a strange decision, to send only one representative; surely a three- or four-person delegation would have given a more rounded view? And Brundage seems to have made up his mind even before he arrived in Berlin. Already harbouring ambitions for a place on the IOC itself (something he would achieve at the 1936 Games), and having already talked with Baillet-Latour about the best way to bring round his American colleagues, he now wrote an article for the AOC's official publication in which he said that holding the Games in Germany 'will mark one more step forward toward the goal of those leaders of amateur sport who carry the hope of developing a better human race through the influence of the Olympics'. The *New York Times* of 26 August 1934 quoted Emmanuel Celler, the Democratic Congressman from New York and an outspoken defender of Jewish interests: 'The American public demands that you [Brundage] at least withhold your judgement until you know the facts.'

Brundage's opportunity to discover those facts had come on a six-day trip to Germany, when he was already in Europe on IAAF business. Accompanied for the most part by Ritter van Halt, whom

The Kaiserhof Hotel in Berlin – a venue much favoured by the Nazis – where Avery Brundage met Jewish sports leaders. (*Author's collection*)

he had first encountered when they both competed in the 1912 Games and whose company he had come to enjoy at IOC meetings and the socializing that went on around them, Brundage was given a carefully managed tour. When he met Jewish sports leaders at the Kaiserhof Hotel in Berlin – a venue much favoured by the Nazis – they may have felt at least a little intimidated by the presence of the deputy Reich Sports Leader, Arno Breitmeyer, an avowed anti-Semite who attended the meeting in his SS uniform complete with cavalry boots. The Jewish sports representatives may also have felt uncomfortable at the presence of Sigfried Edström, the Swedish vice-president of the IOC who had already gone on record as saying that the IOC should support their German colleagues in the face of 'international Jews'.

According to an account by Robert Atlasz, director of the German Maccabi movement, Brundage told the meeting that he could only consider discrimination against Jews in sport; anything else was irrelevant to him. He had no problem with Jewish sport being separated from everyone else's, so long as Jews would be considered for the German Olympic team. In America, he said, there was the concept of 'separate but equal'. Even his own club in Chicago did not permit Jews to enrol as members. But they had equal rights when it came to representing America in the Olympics. And that was what mattered. Atlasz, who four years later would settle in Palestine and would later become a member of Israel's Olympic Committee, must have been depressed by what he heard. It is also impossible to imagine how Jewish athletes felt. On the one hand, their organizations obviously condemned anti-Semitism; on the other, they were German citizens and would have had pride in representing their country.

After his carefully guided tour of German sports facilities, and his sterile meeting with Jewish sports leaders, Brundage reported back to the AOC. His superficial assessment of conditions for non-Aryan athletes was enough to persuade his colleagues. On 26 September 1934, the American Olympic Committee's executive voted unanimously in favour of accepting the German OC's invitation to the 1936 Olympic Games. All eyes now turned to the AAU conference in Miami in December 1934. Although the AOC had cleared the way, AAU approval was vital because the organization had to countersign each athlete's eligibility form. A *New York Times* journalist recognized this: 'American participation in Germany without the AAU would be akin to trying to run a horse race without a horse. The jockey might go the distance, but not very well.' In the event, the issue was still not settled. The AAU, believing that Brundage had been too willing to accept what the Germans had told him, and also that the AOC was desperate to get the Games on at all costs, decided to delay its own decision until the following year.

And so far from the matter being quietly resolved then, it was in 1935 that the debate entered its most bitter phase. Brundage's aspirations to become an IOC member had seen him focus on the AOC presidency; his replacement as AAU president now represented an implacable opponent. Jeremiah T. Mahoney, a former New York Supreme Court judge, high-jump champion and member of the New York Athletic Club, had already proved an outspoken AAU president who had lobbied hard for the 1933 boycott resolution. In March 1935, a poll showed that 43 per cent of American were in favour of a boycott. Against this background, the plight of Jews and other non-Aryans in Germany was becoming increasingly worse, culminating in September with the passing of the so-called Nuremburg Laws.

The International Olympic Committee meeting in Oslo in 1935. Germany's hosting of the following year's agenda was now top of the IOC's agenda. (*Author's collection*)

On 3 July, the official SS newspaper *Schwarze Korps* (Black Corps) reported:

> There was criticism of the fact that in Berlin a group of Jewish women competed with a group of sports women of the police sports clubs of Berlin. We have investigated this fact and are glad to announce that all the members who have participated in this game have been excluded from German sports organizations.

On 6 August, von Tschammer und Osten announced that sports clubs in Germany would set aside the month of October for teaching anti-Semitism. If any of this news reached the USA, it would surely have been a shock for the anti-boycott lobby.

There was also a shock awaiting Charles Sherrill. Brundage thought that the inclusion of a Jew in the German team would probably be enough to win the day. On 24 August 1935, Sherrill saw Hitler in Munich. Their meeting lasted for an hour, during which time Sherrill asked that the Germans include at least one Jew. Hitler insisted that IOC agreement simply meant that Jews could compete for visiting teams. If it was now saying that Jews must be included in the German team, then the Fatherland would stage its own 'German Olympics'. Sherrill's triumph, which had lasted ever since the Vienna conference of 1933, had been shattered in just sixty minutes. He wrote to Baillet-Latour, urging him to meet personally with Hitler and warning him: 'you are in for the greatest shock of your life'.

In October, Mahoney visited Columbia University in search of further support. After Mahoney had spoken, the African-American sprinter, Ben Johnson, told a student gathering that he would not support the boycott because he felt that conditions for blacks in the South were as reprehensible as those for Jews in Germany. 'It is futile and hypocritical that Judge Mahoney should attempt to clean up conditions in Germany before cleaning up similar conditions in America,' said Johnson. In December, on the eve of the AOC annual meeting, Johnson, along with fellow black athletes Jesse Owens, Cornelius Johnson, Ralph Metcalfe and Eulace Peacock, wrote to Avery Brundage favouring American participation in the Berlin Games. That was understandable. While they naturally abhorred racial discrimination themselves – and they were experts when it came to being on the receiving end – African-Americans did not see why they should suffer when it came to the Games. One of the few ways in which their community could advance was through sport.

Glad though he would have been for the support of America's black athletes, Brundage had already taken a huge step forward by circumventing the need for the AAU to endorse competing competitors' Olympic papers. Presumably Baillet-Latour, the pro-Berlin Games IOC president, and Edström, his deputy who felt that they should stand up to 'international Jews', took little persuading to dispense with AAU approval and agree that, instead, Brundage's signature alone, on behalf of the AOC, would be sufficient, given the difficult circumstances. That overcame the technicalities, but it would still be better if the AAU voted to compete in Berlin. Brundage published a pamphlet entitled 'Fair Play For American Athletes' – ironically, the pro-boycott movement was calling itself the Committee on Fair Play in Sports – which asked why the 'birthright' of American athletes to represent their country at an Olympic Games should be jeopardized just because Germany did not want Jews in its own team. Mahoney's committee responded with its own pamphlet entitled 'Germany has Violated the Olympic Code'.

In October, *The Nation*, the official publication of the American Federation of Labor pulled no punches:

> By historic precedent the Games must never be political in character. They are in no sense a government function, but a meeting of the amateur athletes of all nations, managed by international athletic committees. It was hardly to be expected that Adolf Hitler would maintain the non-political character of the approaching contest. Presuming as he does to regulate by government fiat every aspect of the life of the German people, it is not surprising that he should be pictured on an official calendar of the German Olympic Committee with the slogan: 'I summon the youth of the world.' But it is clear that if Herr Hitler is summoning the world's youth to the Olympics, the world's youth may be justified in declining ... No other single gesture could more forcibly bring home

An American Boy Scout raising funds for the country's Olympic team for Berlin. (*Author's collection*)

to the Nazis the disgust of other nations with their programme of repression and brutality.

Two men had already made up their minds not to compete in Berlin. In 1935, Milton Green had four times equalled the world indoor record in the 45 yds high hurdles (the following year he would match the world indoor mark in the 60 m high hurdles). Although as captain of the Harvard team he was one of the leading American collegiate track stars of the era, Green was also Jewish. Along with his Harvard teammate, Norman Cahners, he made it clear that, in support of the US movement to boycott the Games, he would not attend the final US trials.

There was one final voice to be added to this noisy debate. On 27 November 1935, shortly before the AAU conference in New York, the *New York Times* published a letter from Ernest Lee Jahncke, a member of the AOC since 1926, and an IOC member since 1927. Jahncke, a former international yachtsman and Assistant Secretary of the Navy in Herbert Hoover's administration, was the son of German Protestant immigrants. His letter was addressed to the IOC president, Count Ballie-Latour: 'Neither Americans, nor the representatives of other countries, can take part in the Games in Nazi Germany without at least acquiescing in the contempt of the Nazis for fair play and their sordid exploitation of the Games.' It was Jahncke's first public pronouncement on the boycott issue. His reward was to be removed from the IOC at the 1936 Games; his replacement was Avery Brundage.

There were several crucial developments that swayed the 'don't knows', not that there appear to have been many people without an opinion. One of the most significant was probably the case of Olympic fencer, Helene Meyer, German-born to a Jewish father and a Christian mother. She was only 14 when she won the German foil championship in 1924; four years later she took gold in the Amsterdam Olympics, winning eighteen bouts and losing only two. By 1930 Meyer had won six German championships and was world foil champion in 1929 and 1931. In the 1932 Games in Los Angeles she could finish only fifth because of illness and, after being expelled from her Offenbach Fencing Club in 1933 because of her Jewish ancestry, decided to remain in California to study. Now it was suggested that Meyer would be selected for the German team (as her mother was not Jewish, neither was she, although such technicalities did not normally bother the Nazis). In a radio broadcast, the exiled author Thomas Mann, then living then in Pacific Palisades, California, begged her to boycott the Games but, it was reported, she felt it might enable her to regain her German citizenship. Despite Hitler's reaction, Charles Sherrill had probably paid a significant role in Meyer's inclusion, suggesting as he had that a Jew in the German team would do much to solve Sherrill's difficulties back home.

There was also news that the Jewish Gretel Bergmann, Germany's national women's high-jump champion, who had been invited to one of the training camps, would also be included. After being expelled from her athletics club in Ulm in 1933, Bergmann had trained briefly with the Stuttgart branch of Der Schild before going to live in England. She won the 1934 British championship, but facing threats to her family if she did not return home to compete for Germany, Bergmann complied. Rudi Ball, who was half-Jewish, had been included in Germany's ice hockey team for the Winter Games. All this gave the anti-boycott lobby a boost – Germany would consider Jews; here was the proof.

And all this time, George Messersmith, who in March 1934 had been appointed America's minister to Austria, cautioned against believing anything the Germans said on the matter; Lewald was no independent voice (privately, he had asked Messersmith to imagine the consequences for him if he had admitted that there was discrimination against Jewish athletes); everything coming out of Germany was simply a smokescreen. Messersmith constantly warned the State Department against American participation. It seems, however, that the plight of Germany's Jews and other non-Aryans paled into insignificance against the importance of not disrupting the Olympic Games.

On the eve of the AAU conference at New York's Commodore Hotel, the executive committee voted to leave the vote to the floor, without a recommendation from the executive itself. The voting procedure was complex, with AAU districts (three votes each) and associated sports bodies (one vote each) all being allowed a say. Some districts had more than three delegates, however, and in that case the votes were split. The pro-boycott lobby appears to have had most support from the districts. Brundage gathered his support from the affiliated sports organizations. The debate lasted for most of the day, amendments were put forward, and then the final vote was taken. It was narrow. Those against the boycott had won the day by $58\frac{1}{4}$ to $55\frac{3}{4}$. America was going to the 1936 Olympic Games. What the result would have been had delegates known that, just after the American team sailed for Europe, Gretel Bergmann would be told that she was not good enough after all, we will never know.

Chapter Five

BEST INTERESTS OF SPORT

A full two years before the Berlin Olympics, some British sportsmen were already seeing for themselves the changes that had overtaken Germany, and how sport and politics were inexorably intertwined in the Third Reich. In May 1934, Derby County, then a leading team in the top flight of English football, made a four-match visit to Germany. By train to Dover and then a cross-Channel steamer to Ostend, the Derby party eventually reached the German border to find a country swathed in the swastika emblem; the Nazi state was firmly established. Dave Holford was then a 19-year-old outside-left from Scarborough, excited to be included in the tour party despite his lack of experience. He was also staggered by what he saw in Germany.

> Everywhere we went, the swastika was flying. If you said: 'Good morning,' they'd reply with 'Heil Hitler'. If you went into a cafe and said, 'Good evening,' they would respond with 'Heil Hitler.' It was a country where everything had a military overtone. Even then, it occurred to us that this was a nation preparing for war.

In May 1934, Derby County, then one of England's leading football teams, made a four-match visit to Germany. They were obliged to give the Nazi salute before matches but goalkeeper Jack Kirby (far left) turned his back on the VIPs instead. (*Author's collection*)

Derby played in Cologne, Dusseldorf, Frankfurt and Dortmund, losing three times and drawing once. Twice they conceded five goals in a match and were surprised by the standard of their hosts' game. All agreed, however, that if the football had been hard work, overall the tour had been an enjoyable one. Good hotels and plenty of time to relax and enjoy the scenery were just the ticket after a strenuous English season. There was, though, one overriding blot on the collective memory. Just as the England team would be obliged to do in Berlin, four years later, the Derby players of 1934 were ordered to give the Nazi salute before each game. George Collin, a full-back from County Durham, remembered their dilemma:

> We told the manager, George Jobey, that we didn't want to do it. He spoke with the directors, but they said that the British ambassador insisted we must. He said that the Foreign Office were afraid of causing an international incident if we refused. It would be a snub to Hitler. So we did as we were told. All except our goalkeeper, Jack Kirby, that is. Jack was adamant

The English footballers' reserves and officials found themselves sitting alongside local Nazi Party officials. (*Author's collection*)

that he wouldn't give the salute. When the time came, he just kept his arm down and almost turned his back on the dignitaries. If anyone noticed, they didn't say anything.

So, even in 1934, there were already British sportsmen who found the Nazi regime so odious that they were prepared to snub it in public.

Whether it had any bearing on the varied reactions of British sport to the Nazi regime is a judgement now difficult to make, but while the disgruntled footballers were all working-class professionals – Kirby himself had grown up in the South Derbyshire coalfield – the people charged with Britain's Olympic dreams were all solidly amateur, and aristocratic at that. Viscount Portal, the president of the British Olympic Association, was a good shot, an excellent fly-fisherman and also maintained a stud and yachted. The BOA's chairman, Lord Burghley, was one of Britain's most famous athletes who had won gold in the 400 m hurdles at the 1928 Amsterdam Games and silver as a member of the 4 × 400 m relay team in Los Angeles. Burghley, educated at Magdalene College, Cambridge, and a Conservative MP, was one of Britain's three representatives on the IOC, along with Lord Aberdare, a fine tennis player in his days at Winchester and Oxford, and Tonbridge-educated Sir Noel Curtis-Bennett, a distinguished civil servant whose brother was a famous criminal lawyer. In January 1936, while addressing a lunch given by the British Ice Hockey Association for the American ice hockey team which was on its way to the Winter Games at Garmisch-Partenkirchen, Curtis-Bennett complained: 'There are a lot of well-meaning busybodies who are trying to mix sport with politics.' One assumes that he was not referring to the Nazi Government of Germany.

Meanwhile, the debate in Britain rumbled on. The Oxford University undergraduate magazine *Isis* claimed that the 1936 Olympics would take place in a 'hate-poisoned, crazy atmosphere'. Lord Aberdare responded through the *Oxford Magazine*, long regarded as the official commentator on university affairs:

These Games are entirely in the hands of the International Olympic Committee ... seriously alarmed at the time of the ill-treatment of the Jews ... they got guarantees from the German authorities that German Jews of all nations will be welcome ... Germany will be represented by more Jews than has ever been the case before.

Aberdare's point of view was not shared by another Oxford man, Dr William Temple, a former Balliol student and president of the Union, and now Archbishop of York. Temple, a fierce critic of the Nazi regime throughout the 1930s, attempted to get a letter to Hitler, pleading with him to remember the true Olympic spirit and 'show yourself no less generous than the Greeks ... issue a general act of amnesty for the benefit of all those who are suffering imprisonment for religious or racial reasons'. The BOA immediately distanced itself from Temple's missive, which was sent through the German Organizing Committee and is highly unlikely ever to have been passed on to the Führer.

Besides liberal churchmen like Temple, other voices were now raised against Britain having anything to do with the Berlin Olympics. Newspapers such as the liberal *Manchester Guardian* and the Labour-supporting *Daily Herald* were joined by the Trades Union Congress, whose general secretary, Sir Walter Citrine, became involved in a controversial sporting fixture between England and Germany. Unlike the debate raging in America, the issue of whether to take part in the Olympic Games had been slow to take off in Britain, but at the end of 1935 there came an event which triggered a huge reaction. In December that year, England were due to play Germany in an international football match at White Hart Lane, the home of Tottenham Hotspur, a club which, by an unfortunate coincidence, numbered many Jewish people among its supporters. In mid-October there were reports in British and American newspapers of a young Jewish footballer who had been beaten to death after a game in Upper Silesia. Accounts varied: Edumund Baumgartner was a member of the crowd and had been killed by Nazi supporters at the end of the game; or he had been murdered on the pitch after putting his team, Rybnik, in front against Ratibor. The German chargé d'affaires in London, Prince Bismarck, was summoned to the Foreign Office to explain but instead claimed that the whole thing had been invented by the American press. In late October, an anti-Nazi rally attended by 18,000 people in Hyde Park heard Clement Attlee, the new leader of the Labour Party, warn that what was happening in Germany 'would lead the world to war and destruction'. Again there were demands for the football international to be called off.

The most alarming feature of the game was that over 10,000 German fans would be travelling to London to see their team in action, and they planned to march to White Hart Lane through predominantly Jewish neighbourhoods. The *Manchester Guardian* reported that anti-Nazi supporters were planning to distribute leaflets outside all London's major football grounds, highlighting the Baumgartner business and calling for the England-Germany game to be cancelled. When the newspaper asked the Tottenham secretary for his opinion, he said that it was really none of the club's business. The game was an international fixture arranged by the Football Association, whose attention they had drawn to a number of protest letters received by the club. The Anti-Nazi Council wrote to the FA, pointing out that the Nazis would simply use the game as a propaganda opportunity, while the TUC asked to meet with the Home Secretary.

On 1 December 1935, the *Observer* reported:

Sir John Simon, the Home Secretary, yesterday made arrangements to receive tomorrow a deputation representing the General Council of the Trades Union Congress who had appealed to him to prohibit the match, on the grounds that it was possible the German supporters would pass in procession through London streets on the day of the match. Sir John Simon, in reply to the protest, said he was ready to receive a deputation, but he did not think that interference on the part of the Government was called for, and he stated that the introduction of political feeling into what should surely be a purely sporting contest was most undesirable. Sir Walter Citrine, secretary of the General Council of the TUC, in a further letter to Sir John Simon, said that 'such a large and carefully organized Nazi contingent coming to London might confirm the impression among people in this country that the event is being regarded as of some political importance by the visitors.' Dr Von Hoesch, the German ambassador, called at the Foreign Office in connection with the matter. He discussed it with an official, the upshot of the conversation being that both governments are of the same mind – that the match should be regarded purely as a sporting event.

The British Government obviously already agreed. One month earlier, a Foreign Office official called Ralph Wigram had told the Home Office that 'the match should help to promote friendly relations between our two countries'. This opinion was from the man who was providing Winston Churchill with intelligence about German rearmament. Just over twelve months later, Wigram died in mysterious circumstances, officially from a pulmonary haemorrhage, although there were also suggestions that he had committed suicide because he was deeply depressed by the international situation. Nevertheless, it seems that the Foreign Office wanted the game to go ahead; the Home Office would rather it did not, but did not see how they could prevent it. Their dilemma became even greater when it was announced that von Tschammer und Osten, together with Theodor Lewald and Carl Diem, would visit London in early December, their main intention being to attend the international.

On 1 December, the *Observer* told its readers:

It is possible that a representative of the German Embassy will be present to meet the German football team when they arrive by air at Croydon tomorrow for their match against England at Tottenham on Wednesday. The German players intend to stay four days, leaving the day after the match. A motor-tour of London has been planned for them, and it is also possible that they will watch the King drive in State along the Mall on his way to open Parliament on Tuesday. No recent sporting event has been treated with such high seriousness in Germany as this match. Cheap trips to London and back – 60 marks (£3 at par) – have made it possible for 10,000 Germans to travel to England to see the match. Between 1,600 and 1,800 passengers will disembark from the *Columbus* at Southampton early on Wednesday morning. Three special trains will convey them to Waterloo. After a trip round London and lunch, they will proceed to the football ground. Between 7,500 and 8,000 Germans will travel via Dover, and special trains will bring them to London. A description will be broadcast throughout Germany. Sir Percy Vincent, the Lord Mayor, will attend the match with the sheriffs.

The Foreign Office were sending two representatives to the match itself, but not to the official dinner at the Victoria Hotel, given in the Germans' honour by the FA. There would be no royal presence either. The Prince of Wales had told the German ambassador that he would attend, but in the event he was not among the crowd of 54,000 who saw England win a good-natured, sporting game by three goals to nil as the Union Flag and the swastika fluttered side by side over White Hart Lane's main stand. Before the game there had been fourteen arrests for insulting behaviour outside the ground, all of them people demonstrating against Nazism. The 10,000-strong German contingent were impeccably behaved.

At the post-match banquet, Sir Charles Clegg, the FA chairman, clearly irritated, chose to criticize the TUC. The following day, Sir Walter Citrine lashed back:

> So far as the remarks about perverting football into politics are concerned, the trouble is that Sir Charles Clegg does not bother to inform himself of the nature of sport in Germany. If he did, he would realize that football there is part of the Nazi regime.

Citrine also issued a pamphlet, pointing out that Felix Linnemann, head of the German FA, held his job only at the whim of the Reich Sports Leader. The FA secretary, Stanley Rous, wrote later: 'If the Government of the day does not stop a match, how can sporting bodies grade the character and politics of another country?'

Olympic year dawning, and the political furore surrounding the football international over, those hoping for a smoother passage towards Britain sending a team to the Berlin Games were soon to receive a rude awakening. On 7 March 1936, one month after he had officially opened the Winter Games at Garmisch-Partenkirchen, Adolf Hitler violated the Treaty of Versailles and the Locarno Pact by sending German military forces into the Rhineland and occupying the hitherto demilitarized buffer zone between Germany and France. It was Hitler's most blatantly provocative act so far, one daring the international community to react. So far as the Summer Games were concerned, there was inevitable concern in France. How could a nation which had already suffered dreadfully at the hands of Germany in one devastating war, take part in the world's greatest sporting festival in Berlin when German soldiers were again poised on her borders?

The crisis can be measured by the words of Britain's Foreign Secretary, Sir Anthony Eden, who, the following day, wrote:

> We must discourage any military action by France against Germany. A possible course which might have its advocates would be for the Locarno signatories to call upon Germany to evacuate the Rhineland. It is difficult now to suppose that Herr Hitler could agree to such a demand, and it certainly should not be made unless the Powers who made it were prepared to enforce it by military action.

Paris Soir suggested that a boycott of the Berlin Games would not only serve to embarrass Germany, it would also cost the Nazis several million pounds in foreign currency. In the corridors of the

League of Nations, the idea of a boycott was again floated, while several British newspapers suggested that the Games could not now go ahead. The *Daily Telegraph* went so far as to claim that the Summer Olympiad was about to be cancelled, but the British Olympic Committee countered swiftly with a rebuttal.

Indeed, ten days after Hitler's march into the Rhineland, the BOC made a public appeal in *The Times*, asking for funds to send its athletes to Berlin. Over the signatures of the Lords Portal, Aberdare and Burghley, and Sir Noel Curtis-Bennett, it read:

> The British Olympic Council are convinced that in sending a team to Berlin they are acting in the best interests of sport. The Olympic Games have always stood for the ideal of harmony and reconciliation between nations, and it would be nothing short of a calamity if, at this very critical stage in world affairs, this country, to whom the world so often looks for a lead, were not fully represented.

Other members of the BOC simply just did not like the way the Nazis had 'professionalized' Olympic sport. Sir Arnold Lunn, whose family owned the Lunn travel agency which became Lunn Poly, was the 'father of alpine ski racing'; in fact, he was the man who invented the slalom. Lunn led the British team to the Winter Games. The British were amateurs, in contrast to the German team which was sponsored by the state. This angered Lunn. 'There are still some people who ski just for fun,' he told the German media.

Indeed, in 1936 all British Olympic sport was 100 per cent amateur. Even top-flight track and field athletics, which for many years had been opened up to the working class, remained staunchly amateur. Although there were plenty of prizes such as canteens of cutlery and clocks for the winners of meetings all over the country, its ranks remained officially unpaid. Two weeks after the German reoccupation of the Rhineland, the Amateur Athletic Association held its annual meeting in London. One of the AAA's affiliate members was the National Workers' Sports Association (later, the British Workers' Sports Association) which had been founded at a meeting at Transport House, headquarters of the Labour Party, on 26 July 1930. The NWSA tabled a motion calling for Britain to withdraw from the Berlin Games. This time the mood was different, almost certainly due to the situation in the Rhineland; Hitler's trampling over international agreements had brought his regime into sharper focus still. Now there was hardly a speaker at the AAA meeting who did not harshly criticize Germany. Yet the question of whether Britain should actually boycott Berlin was still one that agonized most delegates. Britain had just been to Germany to participate in the Winter Games, so not to take part in the Summer Games would be inconsistent, and probably pointless. The *Manchester Guardian* reported the feeling that isolating Germany at this time would surely be a dangerous move; tact was needed, not an increase 'in the bitterness which she at present feels for her neighbours'. One proponent of Britain's continued involvement was the Jewish sprinter, Harold Abrahams, who had won gold at Paris in 1924. The former Cambridge University student felt that Britain's presence at the Games could have only a positive effect on the delicate international situation. The NWSA agreed to defer a vote on their motion; when it was finally taken, at an extraordinary general meeting in May, it was defeated by 200 votes to 8.

The position of the AAA, the British Olympic Committee and the British Government was that, while obviously it would have been much better if the Games had not been awarded to Berlin in the first place, it was now far too late to do anything about it. In any event, if they themselves boycotted Berlin simply because they did not agree with the politics of the host nation, then how could the British position be that sport and politics must not be mixed? Of course, this might be seen as a convenient get-out clause: when the host nation's politics included banning athletes simply on the grounds of their religion or colour, did not morality have to be taken into account?

There was also an irony in that, had Berlin not been awarded the 1936 Games, then they would have gone to Barcelona. After the effects that Nazism was having on Germany became clear, several 'counter Olympics' were planned by those favouring a boycott of Berlin. In Spain, an *Olimpiada Popular* (People's Olympic Games) was planned for Barcelona. The idea was supported by the left-wing coalition, the Popular Front, after its success in the Spanish elections of early 1936. No Spanish athletes would be sent to Berlin. Instead they would compete in their own Games, the cost of which would be shared by the Spanish Government, the regional government of Catalonia and the city of Barcelona. Foreign teams would be accommodated in hotels constructed for the Barcelona World's Fair in 1929. The Barcelona Games were scheduled for 19–26 July.

A few days before these Games were due to begin, almost 6,000 athletes had been registered from twenty different nations. Spain had registered more than 4,000 competitors, France had sent a large team, and other participating nations included the

USA, Great Britain, Holland, Belgium, Czechoslovakia, Denmark, Norway, Sweden, Palestine and Russia. Teams were effectively representatives of workers' sports associations. In the American team was Bernard N. Danchik, a gymnast and a clerk with the Bookkeepers', Stenographers' and Accountants' Union in New York City. He was also a member of Rabbi Wise's Committee for Fair Play in Sports. Danchik sailed to Spain with a team of eight other American athletes, most sponsored by their trade unions. On 19 July, four days after their arrival, they were awakened by the sound of gunshots outside their Barcelona hotel. Rather than competing in the alternative Olympic Games, they had become eyewitnesses to the outbreak of the Spanish Civil War.

On the third day of fighting, the athletes marched through the streets, demonstrating their support for the people's militia that had risen up against the army led by the fascist General Francisco Franco. When a French athlete was killed, the Spanish Government ordered the evacuation of all foreign teams. The Americans arrived back in New York on 3 August, two days after the Berlin Games had started. Before the team left America, their coach, Alfred 'Chick' Chakin, a physical education instructor at the City College of New York and a former Cornell wrestling champion, had told the *Daily Worker* that the People's Games would be 'a powerful demonstration against fascism'. Some 200 athletes had remained in Spain to fight with the International Brigades, and Chakin returned to join them, enlisting in the Abraham Lincoln Brigade. In 1938, he was captured by troops loyal to Franco and executed. One wonders whether the official Games could have gone ahead in Barcelona, as they would in Berlin, had the Catalonian city been chosen ahead of the German capital. Given that a civil war had erupted in Spain, the answer is surely 'no'; that decision for IOC nations would certainly have been the easier one to take.

On the eve of the official Olympic Games, meanwhile, lingering, and naive, hopes that the Nazis might yet change their attitude had been finally dashed. On 19 June 1936, the white German heavy-weight boxer, Max Schmeling, scored an unexpected victory over Joe Louis, an African-American, in a non-title fight at Yankee Stadium. Schmeling, the 10–1 underdog, annihilated the hitherto undefeated Louis. The German took charge in the fourth round; in the twelfth, Louis was counted out for the first time in his professional career. In Germany, Schmeling was already something of a national sporting hero. Now, after returning home aboard the giant airship *Hindenburg*, he found himself feted wherever he went. Goebbels had laid on a special aircraft to bring Schmeling's wife,

Heavyweight boxer Max Schmeling scored a propaganda point for the Nazis by beating the African-American Joe Louis. But Schmeling was a liberal who later helped Jews to escape from Germany.
(*Author's collection*)

the Czech-born film star Anny Obdra, and his mother to meet him. Then Schmeling was driven to the Town Hall to take tea with Hitler.

In June 1938, Louis would get his revenge, successfully defending his world title against Schmeling on a muggy night at Yankee Stadium. In a 1975 interview, the German recalled that defeat:

> Looking back, I'm almost happy I lost that fight. Just imagine if I would have come back to Germany with a victory. I had nothing to do with the Nazis, but they would have given me a medal. After the war I might have been considered a war criminal.

Louis, meanwhile, could reflect on his treatment by his own countrymen, when members of the American Nazi Party used to visit his training camp daily. 'They would come up with swastikas on their arms … they watched me train and sat around laughing like jackasses,' he wrote. The SS's own newspaper, *Der Schwarze Korps*, was quick to capitalize on Schmeling's 1936 victory: 'The sporting spirit of the great masses of population felt instinctively that our comrade saved the reputation of the white race …'

All this still bothered some members of the British Establishment. In the House of Commons on 22 July 1936, less than two weeks before British athletes were due to parade at the opening ceremony in Berlin, Sir Geoffrey Mander, the Liberal spokesman on foreign policy, insisted that Anthony Eden demand from the German Government an assurance that the Olympic Games would not be used for propaganda purposes. A fellow Conservative, the Ayr MP, Lieutenant Colonel Thomas Moore, jumped to the Foreign Secretary's aid, asking: 'Does the Right Honourable Gentleman not view with disfavour these impertinent pin-pricks to a friendly nation?' Moore was greeted with cries of 'Hear! Hear!' from the Government benches.

Six days earlier, Gretel Bergmann, – who had just equalled the German and European high-jump record of 1.60 metres – had been told that her recent performances had not been good enough to win her a place in the German team after all. At 4.00 a.m. on the day that Bergmann realized she had been used as a pawn in the sick game of Nazi propaganda, police surrounded all Roma encampments in Greater Berlin and transported the inhabitants and their wagons to Marzahn, an open field located near a cemetery and sewage dump in the east of the city, well away from the Olympic complex. Sanitary conditions were poor and contagious diseases soon began to flourish.

Meanwhile, as the youth of the world prepared to converge upon the Third Reich, on 16 July 1936, Victor Klemperer, who the previous year had been dismissed as a professor at Dresden Technical University, under the Law for the Restoration of a Professional Civil Service, had written in his diary: 'And where will we be in two months' times, once the Olympics is over and it is open season on the Jews?'

Chapter Six

THE WINTER GAMES

In the eyes of a largely adoring nation, Adolf Hitler had achieved much for the German people by the early months of 1936: he had reduced the number of unemployed by four million; he had instigated the autobahn programme that would give Germany a major road network unequalled anywhere in Europe; and, like his Italian counterpart, Benito Mussolini, he even had the trains running on time. There was one miracle, however, that even this increasingly Messianic figure could not perform: he could not personally make it snow, and Garmisch-Partenkirchen, venue for the Winter Olympics, was suffering its worst snow drought for a quarter of a century. That year, in a Japanese laboratory, physicist Ukichiro Nakaya was busy producing the world's first artificial snow; but, in early February in Garmisch-Partenkirchen, it seemed that the skiing events would have to be moved to slopes at Elmau and Klais, a few miles to the south; conditions on the bobsleigh run were proving so dangerous that some teams left to practise in St Moritz. Then, on the eve of the opening ceremony, the first flakes began to fall, ushering in a heavy snow storm which created ideal conditions. Clear winter days and frosty nights followed. As the IOC's Official Report commented later: 'The weather was so ideal that one could almost have imagined it had been arranged for by the Organizing Committee.'

Garmisch-Partenkirchen lies about sixty miles south of Munich, on the border between Bavaria and Austria. Originally separate communities on either side of the

The official poster for the 1936 Winter Games suggests a skier giving the Nazi salute. (*Author's collection*)

River Partnach, they were joined under one administration on 1 January 1935. At the same time, the broad, modern Olympia Highway was paved from Garmisch-Partenkirchen to Munich. Garmisch, as the twin towns are now casually called, stands at the foot of the Zugspitze, Germany's highest mountain, and is regarded as a gateway to the Alps. The towns' development into a winter sports area began early in the twentieth century. The first German skiing club was founded in 1905 and a bobsleigh run was opened in 1911. Four years after the establishment of the first cable car in 1926, the rack and pinion mountain railway to the top of the Zugspitze was opened. As the 1936 Winter Games approached, further developments were added, not least the 130,000-capacity Olympic ski stadium at the base of the Gudiberg Mountain. The name of that ski jump, 'Olympiaschanze', dated back further than the 1936 Games, however, and was an act of protest. When Germany was banned from taking part in the 1924 Olympics, Garmisch and Partenkirchen retaliated by hosting the first *Winterkampfspiele* (Winter Tournament) in 1922. It was at the conclusion of this that the ski jump was renamed the 'Olympic Ski Jump on the Gudiberg'. For the 1936 Winter Games, however, the Olympiaschanze had to be completely rebuilt. It reopened early in 1935, with a brand new 142ft-high, 16ft-wide wooden tower for the Olympic special jump, as it was called. The stadium grounds were additionally used as the finishing line for cross-country skiing competitions, and would also serve as the stage for the Games' closing ceremony.

The bob run at the Reissersee, used for the 1934 world bobsleigh championships, was rebuilt for the 1936 Olympics. It was almost a mile long, a natural gully lined with blocks of ice cut from the lake, all surrounded by the barns used to house the bobsleighs and the traces used to transport the sleighs to the starting line. In 1934, an Olympic ice stadium was built in Garmisch, on the other side of the river from the ski stadium. Its wooden stands could accommodate around 12,000 spectators who watched the skating and ice hockey taking place on an artificially cooled rink measuring 100 ft by 200 ft. The whole Olympic complex was tested at the 1935 German national championships. Everything passed with flying colours. German efforts for this, only the fourth Winter Olympic Games, had put those of Lake Placid in 1932, firmly in the shade.

Yet even before the Games began, there were boycott talks again. This time, however, they centred not around the plight of non-Aryan sportsmen and women, but on something much more mundane. The 1936 Winter Olympics were the first to include Alpine races, and the first to have women's races, although the IOC

The bob run, almost a mile long, a natural gully lined with blocks of ice cut from the Reissersee. (*Author's collection*)

insisted that the eighteen medals – three each for slalom, downhill and combined for both men and women – normally awarded in world championships were far too many when converted to the Olympic standard. There would be only six Alpine medals: three for men and three for women, for the combined slalom–downhill score only. More controversial still was the IOC's decision – after a long dispute with the International Ski Federation – that ski instructors were professionals and therefore ineligible to take part in the Olympic Games. Worst hit were the Swiss and Austrians, whose best Alpine racers worked as leading instructors between competitions. French, German and Italian racers, meanwhile, were supported by government training grants and so technically were not instructors. By that logic, French, German and Italian skiers paid to race were amateurs; Swiss and Austrians not paid to race were professionals. Switzerland and Austria decided to boycott the skiing events altogether.

There was one other matter to take care of before the Games could begin: the removal of all anti-Jewish propaganda from the Olympic area. The official poster for the 1936 Winter Games already suggested a skier giving the Nazi salute. Now signs such as the one which read 'Admission of Jews is Forbidden', which hung at the entrance to a ski club in Garmisch-Partenkirchen, were embarrassing the IOC president, Count Baillet-Latour. The story goes that he demanded they be removed, at least for the duration of the Games, otherwise both the Winter and Summer Games would be called off. Hitler was in no mood to cooperate. This was a central plank of Nazi policy; it could not be changed 'for a small point of Olympic principle'. There were some heated moments before Hitler relented – 'You will be satisfied,' he muttered to Baillet-Latour before stomping from the room – and the signs were taken down. Other accounts give credit for their removal to Charles Sherrill, who warned Baron Peter Le Fort, secretary of the Winter Games, that unless they disappeared the IOC ran the risk of the Americans going home once they had seen them.

It was too late to prevent the American journalist, William Shirer, from writing an article in which he said that anti-Semitic notices had been removed from Garmisch so that foreign visitors would remain unaware of 'the kind of treatment meted out to Jews in this country'. He was also annoyed that Nazi officials had commandeered all the best hotels in Garmisch-Partenkirchen, leaving print and radio journalists to cram into small guest houses on the edge of town. The Americans had sent no sports journalists to the Winter Games, preferring to cover them by using correspondents already based in Europe – Shirer himself was then working for the Berlin bureau of the Universal News Service – and so it was inevitable that politics, not sporting excellence, was going to be their beat.

Meanwhile, whether they were packed with high-ranking Nazis, disgruntled reporters or just some of the thousands of ordinary people who had descended on the twin towns, local hotels and gasthofs had never experienced anything like the scenes of February 1936. The occasional economic booms enjoyed over the centuries, even the burgeoning winter sports trade, had not prepared the townsfolk for this. Today, the permanent population numbers around 28,000; the daytime population may be closer to 50,000 on busy weekends when hotels are fully booked and day-trippers arrive. In 1936, more than 800,000 people visited Garmisch-Partenkirchen for the ten-day Olympic winter festival.

On the morning of 6 February, visitors awoke to find heavy snow falling. The Nazis' influence was everywhere. Swastika banners fluttered in the blizzard; military bands thudded and trumpeted away, their sounds muffled by the ever-thickening blanket of snow; columns of Hitler Youth and the National Labour Service crunched through the streets towards the ski stadium where 65,000 spectators had gathered to greet the 756 winter sportsmen and women of twenty-eight nations who lined up to march past the saluting base where Hitler, bareheaded despite the snowstorm, had already received a rapturous welcome. Then in came the teams. The British wore black armbands as a mark of respect to the late King George V, who had died at Sandringham on 20 January. Like most teams, the British raised their arms in the Olympic salute. This went down well in stadium, being greeted by roars of approval from the thousands who assumed this was the Nazi salute. The Americans, whose flag was carried by the long-distance skier Rolf Monsen, a veteran of three Olympics, decided to take no chances; they favoured the Führer only with a simple eyes-right. That did not go down well with the massed ranks of spectators who responded

The Olympic flame burns on top of a tower that bore a chilling resemblance to the watchtowers around Nazi concentration camps. (*Author's collection*)

with only the faintest applause. Then it was the Americans' turn to feel snubbed.

The climax to the opening ceremony was simple. After Hitler, being mercifully brief, had declared the Games open, on the Gudiberg peak at the height of the ski jump, the Olympic flame burst into life from a stainless steel bowl atop a latticework tower that bore an uncanny resemblance to the watchtowers surrounding Germany's ever-growing number of concentration camps, had any foreigners realized it at the time. Then, with the help of German naval personnel, the Olympic flag unfurled lazily from its pole on the opposite side of the ski run, a single cannon shot echoed around the valleys, and village church bells rang out. Karl Ritter van Halt, the Winter Games president, welcomed the competing nations. And finally, the German skier, Willy Bogner, climbed a small rostrum, which had been decked with fir boughs and the Olympic flag, to recite the Olympic Oath as the flags of all the competing nations were dipped around him. The stage was set for a sporting spectacle.

Yet there was no escaping the true nature of the event. The German military was everywhere and Hitler, who had arrived that

German skier Willy Bogner recites the Olympic Oath, surrounded by the flags of the competing nations. (*Author's collection*)

morning on a special train to Kainzenbad, right next to the ski stadium, had surrounded himself with all the leading figures in the Nazi Party. Goebbels, Göring, Streicher, Frick and the rest, they were all in Garmisch-Partenkirchen as the first day of the 1936 Winter Olympics got under way. They overshadowed the sport, often receiving more attention than the competitors themselves. Yet those members of the world's media present waited in vain for the first signs of political interference. Hitler gave them none. Indeed, he was the almost perfect host and made no political speeches. The IOC report on the Games even went so far as to say: 'The German Chancellor ... lent an air of festivity to various competitions through his presence.'

True, there were some hiccups. The American press, already unhappy with their sleeping arrangements, now complained that they had been given too few seats in the press boxes around the complex; they were quickly allotted more. The Americans' gripe was at odds with the official line: 'In Garmisch, seats, tickets, quarters, the most modern of postal organizations and every type of despatch technique were at the disposal of 400 journalists, without

The Nazi hierarchy was well represented in Garmisch-Partenkirchen. Hermann Göring (far right) is an interested spectator during the ice-hockey tournament. (*Author's collection*)

any difference being made in concessions to the German and foreign press.' The Nazis' aim was to confine news reports coming out of Germany to those covering purely sporting stories at the Winter Games, even to the extent that when, on the opening day of the Games, two Luftwaffe trainers collided over Munich and one fell into the main shopping area, killing several people and badly injuring many others, the disaster went unreported in the German press. The only real hint of a problem for Goebbels's Propaganda Ministry was when several journalists saw German troops on manoeuvres in the hills outside Garmisch-Partenkirchen. German soldiers carrying out military exercises on the Olympic doorstep was a story that could not be suppressed, but, overall, the Nazis kept to their script. They allowed only German photographers to record events and pictures were checked by the Propaganda Ministry before being made available for international distribution.

One story that they were happy to encourage was the inclusion in the German ice hockey team of Rudi Ball, a 26-year-old half-Jew from Berlin. Ball, who had been in self-imposed exile, was one of the best players in Europe. He had made his international debut in 1929 and played for Germany in the 1932 Winter Olympics. After the Lake Placid Games, he had left his club, Berliner SC, to join ECH St Moritz in Switzerland. He was playing for the Milanese club, Diavoli Rossi Neri, when called up by Germany for the 1936 Olympics. The move was seen simply as a sop to the IOC, but it has to be noted that, after the Games, Ball rejoined Berliner and as late as 1938 was playing for Germany in the World Championships.

Although it was ice hockey that was to provide the shock result of the Games, it was inevitably the Scandinavians, in particular the Norwegians, who dominated. Seven of the seventeen gold medals went to the 'hardy sons of this small nation', as the German Railroad Information Office's official account

Ivar Ballangrud of Norway, then regarded as the greatest speed skater of all time, won three gold medals at the 1936 Winter Games. (*Author's collection*)

of the Games called them. Three golds were won by one man alone: Ivar Ballangrud. Then regarded as the greatest speed skater of all time, Ballangrud won the 500 m, 5000 m and 10,000 m races, and was pipped into the silver position in the 1500 m race by only one second from fellow Norwegian, Charles Matthisen. The most spectacular event, the special ski jump, went to Birger Ruud, who had grown up in the Norwegian mining town of Kongsberg.

Ruud had attempted an unusual double, competing in both the Alpine and ski jumping events. The inaugural Alpine contest was the combined ski jumping and slalom. Ruud led the downhill race by 4.4 seconds, but when he missed a gate in the slalom, he was given a six-second penalty and ended up in fourth place. On the closing day of the Games, a crowd of more than 150,000 had gathered in and around the ski stadium to watch Ruud's attempt at a gold medal. A thaw had set in, which made the snow on the ski jump heavy and slow, so that distances of 80 m, achieved in better practice conditions, were now impossible. For competitors, the view from the top of the

Norway's great ski jumper, the diminutive Birger Ruud, whose faultless style earned him a gold medal. (*Author's collection*)

jump would have been breathtaking: down below an ocean of spectators contrasted sharply with the snow-clad backdrop. After watching several unimpressive jumps, the restless crowd fell silent when Ruud's name was put up. The Norwegian stood only 5 ft 5 in tall but possessed a superb physique and, although he jumped only 75 m and 74.5 m, his faultless style earned him a narrow victory over the Swede, Sven Ivan Eriksson, who averaged 76 m. Three weeks later, in a Slovenian Alpine valley called Planica, an Austrian, Sepp Bradl, became the first person to jump more than 100 m. At Garmisch, of course, the Austrians had boycotted the skiing events.

The long-distance races were won by Sweden's Erik August Larsson and Elis Viklund, and Norway's Oddbjörn Hagen, while Finland triumphed in the relay. In the endurance race, Sweden took the first four places, each man finishing the 50 km course in the astonishingly fast time of just over 3½ hours. It was, said the official

The breathtaking view that greeted competitors at the top of the ski jump. (*Author's collection*)

magazine, 'a national triumph without equal in the history of the Olympic Winter Games'.

Sonja Henie, meanwhile, completed the Norwegians' achievements by winning the women's figure skating ahead of Britain's 15-year-old Cecilia Colledge. The youngster was only three points behind Henie at the end of the compulsory competition, although in the voluntary exhibition that followed she looked nervous, quite unlike her performance at the European championships in Berlin earlier in the year. These were the days before the top skaters performed last. Colledge was drawn to skate second of twenty-three competitors, before some of the audience had even arrived, and her chance of gold slipped away when she almost fell; her routine had also been delayed after the wrong music was put on. Yet the youngster had captivated everyone present, not least the leading Nazis. Göring, in particular, could not take his eyes off her. For Henie, it was a third Olympic triumph, after gold in St Moritz and Lake Placid. She had been only 11 when she took part in the

first ever Winter Games, at Chamonix in 1924. After the 1936 Games she turned professional, became a US citizen and performed in ice shows, television specials and made a number of films which often featured her skating. Henie was no stranger to Hitler, having been presented to the Führer at Munich's Ice Palace in 1934. Indeed, the pair seemed to enjoy being photographed together. In the men's figure skating, Austria's Karl Schäfer won his second successive gold. In the pairs, Maxie Heber and Ernst Baier took more gold for Germany.

There might have been another Norwegian skating star at Garmisch-Partenkirchen. Sixteen-year-old Laila Schou-Nilsen held every women's speed skating record from 500 m and 5000 m but, due to the exclusion of women's speed skating from the Olympics, she entered as an Alpine skier. Schou-Nilsen's speciality was downhill, but the only Alpine event was the combined; fifth fastest in the slalom, she ended up with bronze. The gold medal went to a German, Christel Cranz, and another German, Franz Pfnür, took the men's gold. Cranz dominated women's skiing in the 1930s, yet she had been born a long

Sonja Henie, the women's figure skating champion, attracted a large band of followers wherever she went in Garmisch-Partenkirchen. (*Author's collection*)

way from any mountains; in Brussels in fact, to where her parents had emigrated from Hamburg. In 1914, the year of her birth, the First World War erupted and the family moved to Freiburg on the edge of the Black Forest. When she was 4 years old, Cranz tried on her first pair of skis. She was soon on her way to becoming a champion.

The bobsleigh brought victory to two nations which would have otherwise enjoyed no Olympic triumph. In the four-man bob, Switzerland took gold and silver, with Britain gaining a creditable bronze. In the two-man event, the American team of Ivan Brown and Al Washbond edged out the Swiss second bob.

The Swiss four-man bobsleigh team which won gold. At the helm is Lieutenant Pierre Musy, also an accomplished horseman who twice won the Grand Prix of Nations event in Hanover. (*Author's collection*)

The greatest surprise of the Games, however, came in the ice hockey, where the British were crowned the new Olympic champions, albeit with a team which mostly lived and trained in Canada and enjoyed dual nationality. The 1936 Olympic ice hockey tournament saw a record fifteen teams take part. Beside the modern artificial rink at the ice stadium in Garmisch, some matches were played on the natural ice of the frozen Reissersee. After the negative effects of snowfall, and based on their experiences at the world championships in Chamonix in 1930 – the natural ice melted and the later, decisive, matches had to be moved to the Sports Palace in Berlin and to Vienna – the LIHG (Ligue Internationale de Hockey sur Glace) decided after the 1936 Olympics to hold all future international championships only in arenas that provided artificial ice.

There had been controversy even before the first match got under way. Canada objected to the inclusion in the British team of right-winger Alex 'Sandy' Archer, born in West Ham but taken to Winnipeg by his Scottish parents when he was only 3 years old. There he learned to play ice hockey and was twice selected as a Manitoba All Star before returning to England in 1935 to play for Wembley Lions for the next five seasons. The Canadians objected on the grounds that Archer had not been released by their national association. The Canadians also took exception to Great Britain selecting Scottish-born Jimmy Foster, considered by many to be the finest goal tender outside North America's professional National Hockey League. Foster – known as 'The Parson' due to the fact that he had seriously considered a life in the church – had also grown up in Winnipeg. He played for the University of Manitoba before making his name with the Moncton Hawks for whom he had missed only one game out of 220 over three seasons. In the autumn of 1935, Foster joined Richmond Hawks, helping them to the runners-up position in the English National League, in an era when interest in the sport was nearing its peak in Britain. The Canadians' complaints were rejected and both Archer and Foster were cleared to play in Garmisch.

Most of the British team's players had strong Canadian connections. High-scoring Gerry Davey was born in Essex but had learnt to play ice hockey at Port Arthur with Elmwood Midgets after being taken to Canada as a small boy. In 1931, when he was 16, he returned to England with his mother. With the assistance of a London newspaper he joined the Princes club, who played at a rink in Knightsbridge, before he moved on to Streatham two years later after a short spell in Zurich. Jimmy Chappell was a native of

Huddersfield in Yorkshire, but was 10 when he moved to Ontario with his parents in 1925. A centre or right-winger, Chappell, who also represented Canada at cricket, played for Oshawa Collegiates before joining Earls Court Rangers in 1935. Left-winger Johnny 'Red' Coward was English-born but raised in Fort Frances, Ontario, before returning to his homeland in 1935 to play for Richmond Hawks. Defenceman Jimmy Boland, an electrician by trade, who was born in Manchester, first played hockey in Montreal. He returned to England to play for Grosvenor House Canadians in 1933 and by the time of the Winter Olympics was team captain of Brighton Tigers. Edgar 'Chirp' Brenchley was born in Sittingbourne, Kent. Taken to Canada by his parents when he was a small child, he learnt to play hockey at Niagara Falls. After a season with Hershey Bars of the American Hockey League, he had also returned to England to play for Richmond Hawks. Gordon Dailley had actually been born in Canada, of British parents. He, too, came to England to play for Grosvenor House Canadians, and then Wembley Canadians.

Under the captaincy of Carl Erhardt, a 39-year-old defenceman from Beckenham in Kent, Great Britain's greatest moment in ice hockey history was about to unfold in Garmisch. After some impressive displays in the preliminary matches, the British beat Canada 2–1. They took the lead after only forty seconds through Davey, who had got up from his sick bed to play. Canada drew level, but with only ninety seconds of normal time remaining, 'Chirp' Brenchley scored the winning goal. It was the game everyone wanted to see and the ice stadium's official capacity of 12,000 was severely tested; some estimates put the number of people who had wedged themselves in at nearer 14,000. As soon as the match finished, hundreds of spectators poured on to the ice to mob the winners, whose journey back to their hotel became a triumphal possession. Medal placings were decided by positions in a final four-team group, rather than by knockout, and when Great Britain, who had also scored a big victory – 5–0 – over Czechoslovakia, fought out a goalless draw with the United States after three periods of overtime, they were nearly there. The Czechs had also lost 7–0 to the Canadians and 2–0 to the Americans. It remained only for Canada to beat the USA by a one-goal margin and Great Britain became the first team to win ice hockey's three major international titles: world and European championships, and now the Winter Olympics. Jimmy Foster was, at that time, the only Scot to win a Winter Olympics gold medal, a distinction he would enjoy for sixty years until joined by Rhona Martin and her curling heroines in 2002. It had been a close-run thing, however; had the Americans beaten Canada, then they would have had equal points with Britain and, depending on the score of that hypothetical victory, could have taken the gold medal on goal-average.

Finally, the Winter Games had included two demonstration sports: ice stock sport, which is somewhat similar to curling and a great favourite in Germany and Austria; and the military patrol race, in which four-man teams of soldiers, each in full kit and carrying a rifle, skied over a 25 km course, pausing halfway to shoot at targets. Demonstrated at the first Winter Games in 1924, and again in 1928, it eventually evolved into the biathlon event. The patrol race was won, rather surprisingly, by the Italians who got round in just under two and half hours to defeat the fancied Finns (just fourteen seconds behind) and Swedes. It was the Austrians, however, who proved the best sharp-shooters, hitting their targets without missing once.

Yet all this was set against a background of darkening international skies. On the eve of the closing ceremony, the daily

The air filled with the smoke from fireworks and flares, the Olympic flag is borne away by six skiers and the 1936 Winter Olympics are at an end. (*Author's collection*)

newspaper *L'Echo de Paris* reported that anger at German rearmament was the main feature of talks between the French Foreign Minister, Pierre-Etienne Flandin, and the Belgian Prime Minister, Paul van Zeeland. 'Belgian people are alarmed at Germany's warlike preparations,' said the paper.

As if to underline this, the closing ceremony proved every bit as militaristic as the opening of the Games. The Wehrmacht was strongly represented, from the massed ranks of soldiers in their field-grey greatcoats, to the young midshipmen from the Kriegsmarine, who ran up the flags of victorious nations while Karl Ritter van Halt presented the medals. In his civilian clothes, Ritter van Halt looked oddly out of place amidst all the military pomp, especially since every award he handed out was accompanied by the boom of an artillery cannon which reverberated around the mountains before dying away in the far distance. As darkness fell, the sky showed clear and bright, twinkling with a million stars. Then the Olympic flame was extinguished, searchlights weaved a pattern across the sky, and the smoke from fireworks and white flares drifted up into the night. Finally, the Olympic flag was lowered and borne away into the darkness by six skiers.

The official report commented: 'The first act was at an end, and each one said to himself: "And now to Berlin."'

Chapter Seven

THE NAZI OLYMPIA

While the Nazis were still basking in the glory of their well-organized Winter Olympics in Garmisch-Partenkirchen, preparations for the Summer Games in Berlin were reaching fever pitch. The German capital was one Europe's great cities, drawing visitors from all over the world. Usually, the city's main focus was Unter den Linden, the beautiful boulevard that ran through the centre all the way to the Brandenburg Gate. In the spring of 1936, however, everyone's gaze had turned to the new Olympic Stadium and its surrounding complex situated in the Grunewald, the large wooded area on Berlin's western outskirts.

The new stadium had grown out of Berlin's original Olympic Stadium, the one that had waited in vain to welcome the 1916 Games. The pre-war stadium had been designed by the architect Otto March and sited five miles to the west of the city centre, on what was then the northern edge of the Grunewald racecourse, which March had also lain out. The Deutsches Stadion had been opened by the Kaiser in 1913. March – who did not live to see the opening – had sunk it slightly below ground level so as not to obscure the race track, and besides its columns and sculptures, it also included an open-air swimming pool cut into the terracing opposite the main stand. The stadium contained a cycling track 720 yds long, which surrounded a running track 650 yds long. The stadium was designed to hold 32,000 spectators in relative comfort. When Berlin was awarded the 1936 Games, March's Deutsches Stadion was the obvious choice for the main stadium. But in twenty years, and despite a devastating world war, there had been a steady advance in new sports facilities throughout Europe. The 1916 stadium was outdated and March's

Architect Werner March. (*Author's collection*)

son, Werner, together with his brother Walter, drew up plans to modernize it.

There was one major problem to be overcome. The Berlin Racing Association (Berliner Rennverein) had been founded in 1906 to establish a race track in this 'noble' part of western Berlin. Otto March's brief had been to retain the forest character of the area, and when the course was opened in 1908, this he had largely achieved. He had also managed to construct the Deutsches Stadion without ruffling too many feathers. Now his son had to increase its capacity, again without offending the sensitivities of the racing fraternity. The stadium could not expand outwards; the only solution lay inside its walls. Werner March's answer was to lower the arena deeper into the ground and build the extra seating downwards instead of upwards. Fundraising began but the outlook was bleak. Money was to be raised from the 'Olympic penny', a levy on spectators at sporting events; by the special postage stamp; and by the lottery to be run specifically for funding the Olympics. This was all very helpful but the German economy was still much more gloom than boom; the Organizing Committee faced a huge task.

Then, on 5 October 1933, Hitler visited the Deutsches Stadion. Six months had passed since his inaugural meeting with Theodor Lewald and Berlin's mayor, Heinrich Sahm, when he had promised support but, in reality, had many more distractions in the earliest days of his Third Reich. Now the Führer seemed more focused on the Olympics. Accompanied by Lewald, Tschammer und Osten, and Wilhelm Frick, the Interior Minister, Hitler went straight to the large gymnasium of the nearby Deutsches Sportforum (Hall of German Sport), where he viewed models and plans of the new buildings and the remodelled stadium. When told that workmen were lowering the arena floor because the Berlin Racing Association would not permit the stadium to rise any higher, Hitler asked how important the racecourse was. He was told that Berlin had two others: Hoppegarten, thirty miles to the east, a great favourite with Berliners with its 1920s grandstands built in the style of Longchamps and its thrilling six-furlong straight; and Karlshorst, in the eastern suburb of Lichtenberg; the Grunewald course, meanwhile, despite being home to the *Grosser Preis von Berlin*, Germany richest horse race, had been losing money for several years.

That was all Hitler wanted to hear. In that case, he said, the racecourse here should be closed down; the entire site must be handed over for Olympic development – and the complex must be the biggest and the best there had ever been. 'When a nation has four million unemployed, it must seek ways and means of creating work for them,' he told his hosts.

Five days later, at meeting attended by Goebbels, Hans Pfundtner, the Secretary of State for the Interior, Walter von Keudell, the Reich Commissioner of Woods and Forests, and members of the Organizing Committee, the Führer began to expand his idea: a new Olympic Stadium must be built by the Reich, and not of concrete and glass as March had suggested, but of natural stone which would symbolize German strength and the enduring nature of Nazi ideology. It must hold at least 100,000 spectators and there must be one long vista from the approach road (which would mean shifting the stadium's axis 165 yds eastwards). There must also be an open-air theatre, and beside the stadium there must be a vast assembly ground for parades and rallies. He told the meeting that Berlin also needed spacious facilities for the assemblies and traditional festivals 'which are an important feature in Germany's

Aerial view of the Reich Sports Field, showing the huge May Field next to the main stadium. The amphitheatre of the Dietrich Eckart theatre can be seen at the bottom of the picture. (*Author's collection*)

modern development'. Hitler hated Werner March's plans for the redesign. They were not grand enough. If this was the best that Germany could do, then he would cancel the Games.

Almost overnight, Albert Speer, a young and relatively inexperienced architect but a protégé of Hitler's, revised March's design, showing how the structure could be clad in natural stone and the glass eliminated. Since Hitler had apparently said that he would refuse even to enter Werner March's original glass and concrete 'monstrosity', Speer's intervention no doubt saved the day, although Speer himself later wrote: 'I was never sure whether Hitler would have carried out his threat, or whether it was a flash of pique which he often used to get his way.' Certainly, once he had been shown the revised plans, the Führer gave his full blessing to the project, whatever the final cost. This proved a huge relief for the Organizing Committee. Now, far from battling alone, they had the full backing of the German state. Everything they wanted, they could have. Their fortunes had changed overnight. In the *Vossischen Zeitung* newspaper of 16 December 1933, Hitler was quoted: 'On this day, I have given my final approval for the beginning and completion of construction on the stadium grounds. With it, Germany receives a sports arena which is searching the whole world for its equal.'

The Olympic Stadium from the Bell Tower. (*Author's collection*)

And so began a huge project. Inside two years, the Olympic complex in the Grunewald swallowed up 42 million Reichsmarks. Some 2,600 workers from 500 separate companies worked long shifts. Over 21 million cubic feet of earth were excavated. Over one million cubic feet of limestone, granite, basalt, marble and dolomite were brought from all over Germany, and thousands of mature trees were transplanted from other areas of the Grunewald. More than 17,000 tons of cement were poured into the site, which used over 7,000 tons of iron. To increase the stadium's seating capacity, the arena floor was lowered 40ft. Beneath the stands lay more than fifty dressing rooms, as well as administrative offices and first-aid stations. In the passageways, there were restaurants and shops which would sell Olympic merchandise such as postcards and badges, as well as flowers and protection against both sun and rain.

Yet the new Olympic Stadium was only part of the Reich Sports Field complex which altogether covered 325 acres. Along the west end of the stadium lay the *Maifeld* or May Field, an area of almost 28 acres that would stage polo and dressage events and be home to exhibitions, parades and rallies. There was open terracing on three sides, rising up to a height of 62ft, and on the May Field's eastern edge stood four stone pillars named after Germanic tribes: Frisian, Franconian, Saxon and Schwabian. On its western edge, under a three-storey grandstand, was Langemarck-Halle, dedicated to the German youth whose lives had been lost in the First World War, particularly those who had suffered devastating losses at Langemarck, near Ypres, in November 1914. There were twelve pillars in the hall bearing the seventy-six flags of the regiments that took part in the battle. From the midpoint of the hall, a stone tower rose almost 250 ft into the air, with twelve shields bearing the names of the German divisions and their units involved at Langemarck. The tower provided observation points for many of the Games' administrators and journalists, as well as police, fire and medical services. It would also house the Olympic Bell, which would become the symbol of the 1936 Games.

A gap in the western edge of the stadium itself, to be called the Marathon Gate, allowed the Bell Tower to be framed between the stadium's two clock towers – the stop clock on the north tower was then the largest ever built – and it was here that the Olympic flame would be lit.

The open-air swimming stadium was now set at right angles to the main stadium, rather than Werner March's original idea of incorporating it in the stadium, as his father had before him. Over 16,000 spectators could view the swimming events, while some

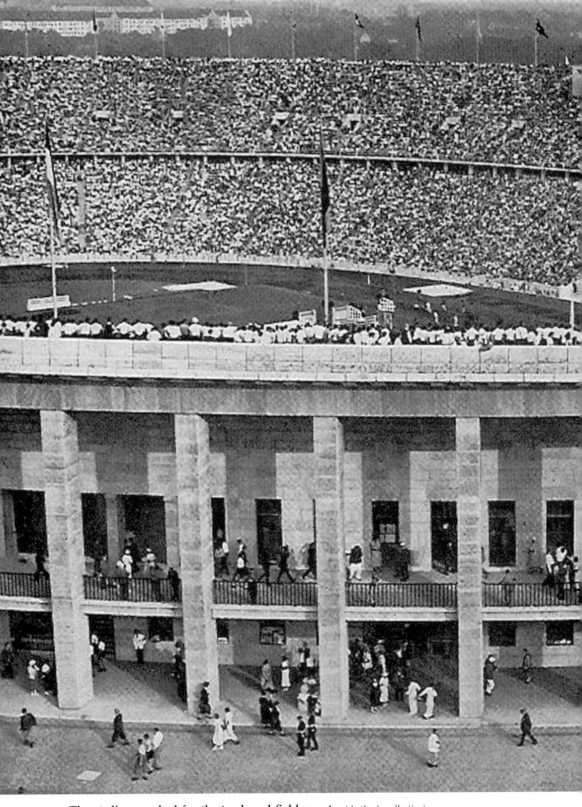

The stadium packed for the track and field events. (*Author's collection*)

The ceremonial plaza leading to the Olympic Stadium through two tall gate towers.
(*Author's collection*)

Looking east from the Bell Tower. (*Author's collection*)

Two views of the Dietrich Eckart theatre, where the gymnastics would be held.
(*Author's collection*)

20,000 could be accommodated in the new hockey stadium. Extensions to the multi-purpose Hall of German Sport housed modern training facilities, while to the north-west of the May Field, dropping away from the Bell Tower, lay something that Hitler had particularly demanded: a spectacular 20,000-seat open-air theatre. Desperately seeking to fulfil the Führer's wishes, March had chosen a bowl-shaped site formed in Berlin's glacial valley. The amphitheatre, designed to mirror the ancient Greek theatre of Epidaurus, was named after Hitler's mentor, Dietrich Eckart, a racist poet, playwright and journalist who had died in 1923. The Olympic gymnastics events would be held here.

The Deutschland Hall on Königsweg was earmarked for the Olympic boxing, wrestling, fencing and weightlifting competitions. (*Author's collection*)

On the eastern side, the whole Reich Sports Field complex was finished by a wide ceremonial plaza, lined with flagpoles, leading to the Olympic Stadium, to a point where stood two 165ft-high gate towers, between which were strung the five Olympic rings representing the five continents of the world. The left-hand tower – the Bavarian Gate – bore a clock; the right-hand tower – the Prussian Gate – a huge swastika emblem. The stadium was a triumph of neo-classicism, but one essentially lacking in beauty. From the very beginning, Hitler had recognized the political value of architecture, and so the sheer Wagnerian scale of Berlin's Olympic venue, with its statues and reliefs celebrating Aryan athleticism, reflected the values of National Socialism and the Third Reich.

A second decision of great importance was made during the autumn of 1933 when Werner von Blomberg, the Reich Minister of Defence, upon the recommendation of the Chief of the Defence Department, Lieutenant General Walter von Reichenau, resolved not only to place the Döberitz barracks at the disposal of the Olympic Committee, but to erect an Olympic Village for the athletes at the military training grounds north of the autobahn to Hamburg and about nine miles from the Olympic Stadium. At Diem's suggestion it was also decided to organize an international youth and student encampment and invite each competing nation to send a group of thirty boys and young men, who would be the guests of Germany during the period of the Games.

The problem of incorporating the Reich Sports Field into the Grunewald district was solved through the creation of a fringe of trees and shrubbery around the entire plot. A new network of streets with seven radial roads of approach was planned, with a 91 ft-long bridge leading to the eastern main entrance of the Olympic Stadium, while a second bridge 58½ feet wide was constructed on the street approach to the western entrance of the May Field; two existing bridges were widened from 38 ft to 94 ft and 104 ft

Members of the Hitler Youth escort the great Olympic Bell to its position at the Reich Sports Field. (*Author's collection*)

respectively. Parking for 8,000 cars was provided at the Reich Sports Field and its immediate vicinity, and German Railways enlarged the two municipal stations in the vicinity of the Reich Sport Field to the extent that 50,000 people could be accommodated in one hour. A new underground railway station was opened.

Finally, there was the Olympic Bell. It had apparently been Theodor Lewald's idea that a gigantic bell should be cast, hung in a tower that would be visible from all around Berlin, and tolled at the opening and closing of the Summer Games. According to the *Official Guide to the Ceremony of the XI Olympic Games in Berlin 1936*, the bell, designed by the Berlin sculptor, Walter E Lemcke, was produced by the Cast-Steel Fabrication Company in Bochum. It weighed over 10 tons and stood 8½ ft tall and 9 ft in diameter. Its clapper alone weighed 15½cwt, and the wooden yoke on which it hung tipped the scales at 3½ tons. Around the rim, in Gothic script, ran the words: *Ich rufe die Jugend der Welt* (I summon the youth of the world). The bell bore two symbols, one on either side: the Imperial Eagle, which held the five Olympic rings; and the Brandenburg Gate. Its design as the symbol of the 1936 Olympic Summer Games had been protected by being registered at the Municipal Court of Berlin-Charlottenburg on 22 June 1933. The *Official Guide* also reported that the Organizing Committee had commissioned the State Porcelain Factory in Berlin to produce small but faithful reproductions costing 4.50 Reichsmarks each. These could be purchased only from authorized shops at the Reich Sports Field, or from the manufacturers. Other miniature 'Olympic Bells' were produced, but they did not correspond exactly to the original.

Porcelain money boxes made in the shape of the Olympic Bell.
(*Author's collection*)

On 16 January 1936, in Bochum, the massive bell was loaded on to a flat-bed truck, originally built to transport a massive granite block to the Tanneberg Memorial where President Hindenburg had been buried the previous year, and supplied by German State Railways. On its stately passage to Berlin, the bell attracted huge crowds. Through Dortmund, Hanover, Brunswick and Magdeburg, it was saluted by the military, and cheered by thousands of schoolchildren. Army bands, factory sirens and church bells welcomed it along its way. In

The Hall of German Sport and adjacent Swimming Hall, which was also used as a temporary medical station. *(Author's collection)*

Potsdam, the mayor gave a speech of welcome. Then it was on to Berlin itself, along the Kurfürstendamm and Charlottenburger Chaussee to the Brandenburg Gate, along Unter den Linden, then into Kaiser Franz-Josef Platz, where the bell was formally handed over to the Organizing Committee. After being exhibited around the city, early on the morning of Monday, 11 May – the date was kept secret so as to avoid a huge crowd gathering – the bell was at last taken to the May Field and, with surprisingly little difficulty considering its weight, raised into position in the Bell Tower. All that was now needed was an Olympiad.

Chapter Eight

ACROSS NATIONAL FRONTIERS

On 18 May 1934, during the thirty-first session of the IOC, held in Athens, Theodor Lewald reported a plan 'thought out by the Organizing Committee, which would consist of lighting the torch on the Marathon Tower with a flame transmitted from Olympia to Berlin'. The minute continues:

> Before asking the concurrence of the Olympic Committees of Greece, Yugoslavia, Romania, Hungary, Austria and Czecho-slovakia to organize the transport by their athletes of the sacred flame across their territories, Dr Lewald wished to communicate the plan to the Committee. The IOC fully approved of his plan.

On the last day of that session, at Olympia itself, the idea was confirmed:

> The Hellenic Olympic Committee handed to the president of the IOC a sacred olive branch which he in turn entrusted to the care of the mayor of Olympia, requesting him to have it sent to Berlin for the opening of the Games of the eleventh Olympiad with the torch which will light a fire on the Marathon Tower.

So began a symbolic Olympic tradition.

Fire had played an important part in the ancient Olympic Games. To the Greeks it was a sacred element, its purity guaranteed by obtaining the flame from the sun's rays, and they maintained perpetual flames in front of their temples. At Olympia, where the ancient Games took place, a flame burned permanently on the altar of the goddess Hestia, situated in the Prytaneum, where feasts were held to honour the athletes at the end of the Games. In Athens, flame races (*lampadedromia*) were held to honour gods, including the rebel Prometheus. The races commemorated the Titan Prometheus' act of stealing sacred fire from the Olympian gods, thus bringing wisdom and knowledge to Man. The flame was carried by runners and the first competitor to arrive at the altar of the god had the honour of renewing its fire. All this would have had enormous appeal to Hitler, who admired the powerful imagery of

Greek gods and wanted the Berlin Games to promote his belief in Aryan supremacy. Indeed, the rite would link the Nazis directly to Ancient Greece, which Hitler believed had been an Aryan paradise full of heroic, blue-eyed blond youth with finely chiselled features.

Yet, contrary to popular myth, so far as the modern Games are concerned, the Nazis themselves invented neither the Olympic flame nor the torch run. Foot races with torches were organized during the International Congress for the Restoration of the Olympic Games held in Paris in 1894. And at the end of the Stockholm Games, on 27 July 1912, Baron Pierre de Coubertin, founder of the modern Olympic movement, had declared:

> And now ... great people have received the torch ... and have thereby unde taken to preserve and ... quicken its precious flame. Lest our youth temporarily ... let the Olympic torch fall from their hands ... other young people on the other side of the world are prepared to pick it up again.

Konstantin Kondylis departs on the first leg of the torch run from Olympia, the first of 335 runners who would carry the flame to Berlin. (*Author's collection*)

A flame had been lit in an Olympic stadium for the first time in 1928, at the Amsterdam Games. It stood atop a tower specially made for this purpose by Jan Wils, whose stadium was designed in a new, functional tradition. 'It gave sports architecture a face', according to the art historian, Maurits Nibbering. Another flame burned at the Los Angeles Games in 1932. At the closing ceremony, a quote by de Coubertin – who since 1925 had been the IOC's honorary president after Baillet-Latour took over the presidency – appeared on the stadium display board: 'May the Olympic torch follow its course throughout the ages for the good of a humanity ever more ardent, courageous and pure.' And at Garmisch-Partenkirchen, for the first time, the Olympic flame was present during a Winter Games. Now, in Berlin, the ceremony would be taken one step further: the flame would be ignited by a torch carried from the site of the ancient Games.

The idea for an Olympic torch run has been almost universally credited to Carl Diem. The general-secretary of the German Organizing Committee had first been associated with a torch relay as long ago as 1922, when students from the *Deutsche Hochschule für Leibesübungen* (German University for Physical Education) staged one to commemorate his fortieth birthday and simultaneously the beginning of the *Deutsche Kampfspiele*, the German national games, born and held in protest at Germany's exclusion from the 1920 and 1924 Olympics. It clearly appealed to Diem and was something he had apparently been thinking about in more detail since the 1932 Los Angeles Games. In December 1933, five months before the IOC approved the idea, Diem had written in his diary about a torch relay held in Bulgaria, when a flame was carried from Preslaw to Sofia.

There is one account of another German being responsible for the 1936 torch run. On 22 May 1934, on the eve of their final session, held at Olympia, IOC members were entertained by the mayor of Tegea, an ancient village in the Peloponnese and home to the temple of Alea Athena. Someone, erroneously named as the Duke of Magdeburg, is alleged to have declared:

> Participants, a thought has just come to my mind and I swear before you that I shall implement it before the beginning of the next eleventh Olympiad to be celebrated, in 1936, in my hometown, Berlin. I want to organize a grandiose relay race between adjacent states during which athletes from these countries will carry to our stadium the Olympic light from the sanctuary of Olympia. It is only right that Greece should once again bring light to the West.

An inspection of the list of IOC members of the time leads one to believe that the speaker was perhaps the Duke of Mecklenburg-Schwerin, who represented Germany, although when the Athens session opened on 17 May, he was listed as absent, having sent his apologies. But certainly no Duke of Magdeburg ever seems to have been associated with the Olympic Games.

Yet another account has Lewald and Diem being 'bewitched by the beautiful scenery, age-old trees and the flowing waters of Ancient Olympia ... so they decided to link the two places, Ancient Olympia and the city where each of the contemporary Olympics would be held'. This account gives Lewald and Diem joint credit, along with their Greek counterparts, Ioannis Ketseas and Alexandros Philadelpheas, for conceiving the idea of lighting the 'sacred' flame and organizing the Olympic torch relay. There is little doubt, however, that Carl Diem was the instigator of, and the driving force behind, what would become a definitive part of the modern Olympics. The matter had already been debated in Germany months before the IOC visit to Olympia. It is certainly difficult to imagine that the thought had 'just come into the mind' of the Duke of Mecklenburg-Schwerin (if it was he) as he gazed on ancient Tegea. Diem was certainly surprised to learn later that the people of Tegea, having heard IOC members discussing the torch relay over lunch on that hot May day, and perhaps encouraged by the duke's claim, had promptly erected a marble plaque declaring their already historic town as the home of the Olympic torch run.

It was probably to Diem's greater annoyance that, back in Germany, William Haegert's Olympic Games Propaganda Commission had already claimed credit for the torch relay. In the official report of the Berlin Olympics there is an account of a meeting of the commission on 8 February 1934:

> The suggestion of Ministerial Councillor Haegert that an Olympic relay should be organized was responsible for the plan of the Secretary-General to hold a torch relay run from Olympia to Berlin, this idea having also been inspired by an antique relief of two Erotes at the Palazzo Colonna in Rome depicting a torch relay run.

Haegert's proposal? Diem had been pushing forward the idea of a torch relay for months, if not years.

Now, however, the issue took on yet another dimension. Perhaps in an attempt to counter Haegert's claim, in his message to the runners de Coubertin planned to omit *any* reference to the relay's German origin. Lewald wrote to the honorary president, insisting that 'it is necessary to say emphatically that the idea and the organization are German'. De Coubertin quickly countered, asking how he could say that Diem was the author 'when an Athenian newspaper has announced that the author of the idea was the Greek archaeologist Philadelpheus'. De Coubertin appeared worried that he would lay himself open to allegations that he was 'too pro-German'. Lewald, in turn, expressed his disbelief that the honorary president's answer was not to mention Germany at all. Not until the day before the first runner was due to leave Olympia was a compromise reached.

Planning for the torch relay had begun in June 1935 when directions and regulations were printed in the languages of the five countries through which the flame was to pass. In September, Werner Klingeberg, a former student of Diem's and now director of the Sport Department of the Organizing Committee, and Pay Christian Carstensen, a member of the Games' Propaganda Commission, travelled to Olympia and then drove back to Berlin along the entire 2,126-mile route, to ensure that every potential problem had been pre-empted. Each of the 3,422 runners was allowed five minutes to cover his own individual kilometre – the route was split into metric sections – and each runner also had to know the next section as well as his own, in case of emergencies. The Organizing Committee estimated that an average of five minutes would be required for each kilometre, and the Olympic Committees of the different countries were authorized to make special provisions such as increasing the stretches in thinly populated sections or allowing more time for negotiating difficult districts. The route would take some runners over passes almost

5,000 ft high and occasionally, in the early stages, along trackways where there was no proper road.

The torches – a new torch would be ignited by each runner – were distributed in March 1936, but only after numerous experiments and trials in order to obtain a torch that would burn for up to ten minutes (in case a runner had to double up) and under all conditions. It soon became obvious that torch holders would be needed, and the Krupp firm in Essen offered to produce these in stainless steel. The original idea had been to imitate the Ancient Greeks, whose torches were made from narthex, a plant found all around Ephesus. When dried, the plant can burn for hours until totally consumed, making it the means by which the ancients transferred fire between hearths. Narthex featured large in Greek myths concerning fire. In Athens, young men wearing nothing but a diadem hung over their foreheads would race in relay teams from the port of Piraeus, south of the city, to the Acropolis, trying to keep a baton made of flaming reeds from the narthex plant alight until they reached the altar of Prometheus. It must have been a hypnotic sight in Classical

The Olympic torch, designed by the sculptor Walter E Lemcke and manufactured by Krupp. (*Author's collection*)

Greece, but in twentieth-century northern Europe, narthex was not the answer. Authenticity would have to be sacrificed for expediency. The Krupp company came up with stainless-steel torches, each 10½ins long, 6ins in diameter and weighing 2 lbs, with magnesium heads that would burn regardless of weather conditions. The torch was designed by the sculptor Walter E. Lemcke, who also designed the huge Olympic Bell. On the holder was the inscription *Fackelstaffel-Lauf Olympia–Berlin 1936* (Torch Run …) with the Olympic rings and the Imperial Eagle super-imposed. On the bottom part was engraved the line of the flame's route from Olympia to Berlin. Also engraved on the holder was the inscription *Organisazions-Komitee fur die XI Olympiade Berlin 1936. Als Dank dem Trager* (… In Gratitude to the Bearer). A plate at the top of the holder protected the runner from flames which might be whipped up by the wind.

In those days of secure European frontiers, customs difficulties also had to be overcome, with special dispensation acquired for the transporting of a chemical element across national borders. Delays also had to be factored in, and an additional two-hour period was inserted for each 80–100 kilometres, the intervals being utilized in the larger cities for special ceremonies. Here the fire would be allowed to 'rest' in a bowl especially prepared for the purpose. In every case, however, the runners had to depart punctually and the entire relay run had to be organized so that the final torch bearer would enter the Olympic Stadium at the precise moment during the opening ceremony.

Special ceremonies in the cities through which the Olympic flame would be carried 'constituted an effective introduction to the Olympic Games', according to the official report. A model programme was sent to each town. This included

> arrival of the runner, ignition of the Olympic flame, singing of the hymn, *Burn, Olympic Flame*, an address by the mayor, general singing, gymnastic exercises by the men, women and children, sporting demonstrations, singing of the Olympic Hymn, festive address dealing with the Olympic Games, folk dancing, folk songs, preparation for the departure of the next runner, words of consecration, singing of the national anthem, departure of the runner, pealing of the bells … Otherwise, the arrangement of the special ceremonies was left in the hands of the National Olympic Committees, who performed their tasks enthusiastically and diligently with the result that impressive national festivals were often organized.

The Olympic torch relay run began at noon on 20 July 1936. The sacred fire was ignited by one of thirteen Greek 'maidens' using a conical mirror, manufactured by the Zeiss optical equipment firm, that concentrated the sun's rays on a wand of kindling. The girls then filed across the grooved flagstones where athletes had begun their races in ancient times, past the Temple of Hera, and into the Altis, Olympia's sacred enclosure, where the first runners were waiting. Here they lit a flame at the altar set at the foot of the Kronos hill, to where the 'stele', or tablet, erected in honour of de Coubertin – now too frail to attend in person – had been brought. A long address from de Coubertin – in which he managed to mention the German Organizing Committee who had 'devised and organized the relay run' – was read out. A cannon boomed across the Alpheios Valley and the Olympic Hymn was sung. Georga Konpulos, the Greek Minister of Education, spoke, and then Herr Pistor, the German chargé d'affaires, declared: 'O fire, lit in an ancient and sacred place, begin your race, and bring greetings to the youth of all the world, gathered together in my country. Bring greetings also to my Führer and to the whole of the German people.'

The first runner, Konstantin Kondylis, wearing only running shoes and shorts, finally ignited his torch and departed on the first leg to Athens. It took 335 runners to transport the flame to the Greek capital, where King George II received the torch in the white marble Olympic Stadium rebuilt for the first modern Olympics in 1896. Surrounded by young Greek women in ancient costume, and by some fifty military personnel, each of whom bore the flag of one of the nations due to compete at the Summer Games, the king lit the flame on an altar.

This ceremony at Olympia had been broadcast around the world, and in Berlin, the State Commissioner for the capital, Dr Julius Lippert, another extreme anti-Semite, organized a celebration in front of the town hall, the wireless broadcast from Olympia forming an essential part of the programme. Now, hourly reports about the progress of the relay run would arrive at the Organizing Committee's headquarters, and as the Olympic flame neared its goal 'the enthusiasm increased throughout Europe', according to the official report. The German broadcasting team were to face many difficulties along the route, beginning, not least, with the fact that Greece itself had no broadcast network. The road surfaces were often appalling, and occasionally made even worse by torrential rain, while temperatures could soar into the high 90s in the blistering summer sun of southern Europe. From Athens, runners took the flame to Delphi and into Salonika, into Bulgaria – to Sofia,

where the flame burned in front of the cathedral, and Zaribrod –
and then across the frontier into Yugoslavia. From Nis, the birth-
place of Constantine the Great, the torch was carried to Belgrade
and then to Novisad on the Danube. For some of the way it was
carried along the line of the Orient Express railway. In Belgrade, the
ceremony around the flame was also used to mark the assassination,
by a Macedonian activist in Marseilles two years earlier, of King
Alexander I; the king had been on a state visit to France to
strengthen an alliance against Nazi Germany.

The flame was borne across Hungary by way of Szeged on the
Tisza River, to Budapest – where it was received in front of the
tomb of the Unknown Soldier – and Oroszvár. As it made its way
across the Great Hungarian Plain, gypsies heralded the torch with
their own special brand of music; in Berlin, its final destination,
other gypsies were already being rounded up and thrown into
camps.

On towards the Austrian frontier, the flame was carried aloft. At
the border, the fire was accepted by the president of the Austrian
Olympic Committee, Dr Theodor Schmidt, a balding, corpulent
figure dressed in white tracksuit trousers who looked out of place
as he carried the torch the first kilometre into his country. From
Karlburg, the torch arrived in Vienna on 29 July. It was due in the
vast Heldenplatz, the square with its equestrian statues that is
one of Austria's symbols of national identity, at 8.00 p.m. Well
before then, the square was packed with people wanting catch a
glimpse of the Olympic flame. At the nearby Hofburg Palace, for
six centuries the seat of Austrian government, there was a crowd of
ragged-looking young men with a different motive: local Nazis
had decided to seize this Olympic moment to stage the biggest
demonstration against the Austrian Government to date. Police
units looked on as the German national anthem filled the air; and
when the gold medal skater, Karl Schäfer, finally bore the torch
through the gates of the Hofburg, into the spectacular setting of the
floodlit square, cries of 'Heil Hitler' reached a crescendo.

**(Opposite page) Dr Theodor Schmidt, president of the Austrian Olympic
Committee, carries the Olympic flame for the first kilometre into his country.**
(Author's collection)

Postcard advertising the arrival of the Olympic torch in Vienna. (*Author's collection*)

After the fire altar had been lit at the palace gates, Dr Schmidt addressed the crowd, but at the mention of Wilhelm Miklas, the Christian Socialist president of Austria, a storm of booing and catcalls erupted; Miklas, a hated figure, had stubbornly refused to hand over elements of government and public services to Austrian Nazis. When Prince Ernst Rüdiger Starhemberg, the vice chancellor and Minister of State Security, stepped forward, the crowd's rage reached a new intensity. Although he had taken part in Hitler's failed Munich beer hall putsch of 1923, Starhemberg had also worked hard to make Austria an independent fascist state, fervently opposing the Austrian Nazi Party and their support of a union with Germany. His speech was drowned by enraged Nazis and although President Miklas himself was received in silence when he spoke, when Starhemberg ignited his torch to set off on the next stage of the relay, he was met by a wall of hatred from the thousands of Nazi supporters who had lined the first part of his route. In the same way, those Austrian athletes at the ceremony who were known to be against the Nazi cause were roundly booed. If there was anyone still of the opinion that the Olympic Games and politics could be kept apart, they would have had their illusions rudely shattered on that warm summer's evening in Vienna.

Leaving the explosive atmosphere of the Austrian capital behind, the Olympic flame proceded to the independent city of Waidhofen an der Ybbs in Lower Austria. Then into Czechoslovakia: through Tábor and its kaolin mines; Prague, the capital since the country's formation in 1918, where it was welcomed at the Huss monument in the old town; and then to the industrial city of Teplice near the German border. It entered the Fatherland by the Hellendorf-Peterswald Pass, where 50,000 Germans had swarmed into the village of Hellendorf to see the exchange made – after a firm handshake between the runners – at just before midday on Friday, 31 July. Now on German soil, the flame was saluted every inch of its way to Berlin. From Dresden, runners took it thirty-seven miles north-west, through Meissen, Wainsdorf, Krauschütz, Elsterwerda-Biehla, Haida and Zeischa, to Bad Liebenwerda. The town had prepared well for the flame's arrival; the Olympic rings were fixed to the Lubwartturm, a famous local tower which was floodlit for the occasion.

That day, a meeting of the International Sporting Press Congress was taking place in Berlin. In the afternoon there was an elaborate programme of exhibition and stunt flying at Tempelhof airfield, and in the evening Theodor Lewald was host to 430 guests at a banquet held in the White Room of the Charlottenburg, the former

The Olympic flame is carried past the massed ranks of German youth organizations and on towards the fire altar in Berlin's Lustgarten. (*Author's collection*)

The last leg of the journey, from the Lustgarten to the Olympic Stadium. (*Author's collection*)

royal palace. At midnight it was reported that the Olympic torch was on the last leg of its long journey.

Through the torch run, Carl Diem had tried to combine the Olympiads of Ancient Greece with the modern Olympic Games. It was certainly a symbolic gesture which had generated intense excitement throughout Europe. The official report waxed lyrically: 'A new Olympic symbol and ceremony had come into being, surmounting all differences of opinion and many major obstacles and reaching across national frontiers ...' That was a generous sentiment.

Chapter Nine

LET THE GAMES BEGIN

If Saturday, 1 August 1936 had dawned dull and damp, it did little to spoil the opening day of the Summer Games for the tens of thousands of Berliners and visitors who awoke to find the German capital already in triumphal mood. From first light, the streets reverberated to the sound of marching feet as German Army units took up their positions for the ceremonials to be performed that morning; then military bands began to strike up. Just like the opening day of the Winter Games in Garmisch-Partenkirchen six months earlier, no one was left in any doubt about the militaristic nature of the 1936 Olympics.

Esther Myers, a 20-year-old student schoolteacher from Kansas, was visiting Europe that summer. From Berlin, where she had arrived on the eve of the Games, she wrote to her local newspaper, the *Douglass Tribune*:

> We found Berlin in festive mood. The great Unter den Linden was bordered on either side by the Nazi flags, posters of German towns, and the flags of the fifty-two nations who had entries in the activities. The buildings were draped with flags and greenery.

Myers would no doubt have witnessed the scenes along the six-mile long Via Triumphalis which ran from the magnificent square of the Lustgarten, through Unter den Linden, Charlottenburger Chaussee, Bismarck Strasse, Kaiserdamm, Adolf Hitler Platz and Heer Strasse to the Olympic Stadium and along which thousands had been camped out all night. If she had been on Unter den Linden at 8.00 a.m., at Pariser Platz near the Brandenburg Gate, she might have seen the band of the Wachtruppe Berlin, the Berlin guards regiment, drawing up outside the Grandhotel Adlon, the premier hotel in Germany which had been opened in 1907 by Kaiser Wilhelm II. For the duration of the Games, the Adlon was used as the IOC's headquarters as well as that of a ladies committee formed to offer 'lady relatives of the guests of honour the opportunity of becoming acquainted with Germany and her people', and boasting Frauen Göring, von Tschammer und Osten and Pfundtner among

Unter den Linden, all dressed up for the first day of the Olympic Games. (*Author's collection*)

its members. Now lady and gentleman guests alike were roused by a stirring rendition from the band, which then marched off east along Unter den Linden to the Lustgarten before returning to barracks in Rathenower Strasse by the same route, having completed its task of waking up central Berlin.

Throughout the city there was huge activity. Between 9.15 and 10.30 a.m., the Army Carrier-Pigeon Institute based at Spandau transported 20,000 birds in 100 vans to the Olympic complex and placed them in their cages along the south and north walls of the May Field and in the stadium itself. At 9.30 a.m., IOC members set out from the Adlon for religious services, Protestants proceeding to Berlin Cathedral in the Lustgarten, Catholics to St Hedwig's Cathedral. At 9.45 a.m., 1,000 members of the International Physical Education Students' Encampment, and 780 members of the International Youth Encampment, arrived at the war memorial, followed by honour battalions from the German Army, Kriegsmarine and Luftwaffe. At just after 11.00 a.m., Baillet-Latour, on behalf of everyone who was about to take part in the Games, laid a wreath at the memorial in honour of those who had been killed during the First World War.

All this time the torch runners had been nearing Berlin, their route lined by thousands of spectators, in villages and towns, and on the roads in between. Not long before midday, the torch reached the southern suburbs of the capital on the Gross-Beeren–Berlin autobahn; just over an hour later, it was carried into the Lustgarten at the eastern end of Unter den Linden, just under eight miles from the Olympic Stadium itself. The former Berlin City Palace garden, and later pleasure grounds, had been converted into a military parade ground by the Nazis. For this special day, the Lustgarten had been left in the hands of Albert Speer, who dressed it with 20 ft-long swastika and Olympic banners. Large stands had been erected and, in front of the palace, an altar had been built to receive the flame. The German Organizing Committee had planned a special programme for that morning, climaxing with a ceremony in the Lustgarten involving 25,000 German youngsters as well as youth groups from twenty-eight other nations.

Members of the government addressed the huge crowd: Baldur von Schirach, who had destroyed all independent youth organizations or caused them to be absorbed into the Hitler Youth; Hans Tschammer und Osten, the former SA man whose organization had murdered German sportsmen and women; Joseph Goebbels, the man charged with camouflaging, for the duration of the Olympics at least, the brutal outrages being perpetrated against non-Aryans;

The Lustgarten, decorated by Hitler's favourite architect, Albert Speer. Some 25,000 young people wait as the official guests arrive. (*Author's collection*)

Bernhard Rust, the Education Minister who had ordered that Jews be expelled from youth and welfare organizations. They all now gave a hearty welcome to 'the youth of the world'. Then a fanfare of trumpets announced the approach of the Olympic flame. It was carried past the massed ranks of German youth to be heralded by the uniformed government officials standing on their dais, who flung up their arms in the Nazi salute.

At 1.00 p.m. – precisely the appointed time – the runner dipped his torch to ignite the fire altar in front of the palace. Now a huge public choir sang the German national anthem *Deutschland über Alles*, and then there were spirited renditions of the *Horst Wessel Lied* (Horst Wessel Song), the anthem of the Nazi Party, chosen to glorify Wessel, a violent activist murdered in 1930, as a martyr. After its twelve-day journey from Greece, the Olympic flame had been received in Berlin. Now it had to be carried a little further still, to the Olympic Stadium where thousands already waited.

Members of the IOC leaving Berlin Cathedral in the Lustgarten. (*Author's collection*)

As the crowded Lustgarten had watched the arrival of the Olympic flame, Adolf Hitler had entertained members of the IOC to lunch at the Reich Chancellery in Wilhemstrasse. First Baillet-Latour, standing a few feet in front of the Führer, in a long speech praised German efforts. He ended:

> I feel certain that the stupendous preparations which Germany has made for the Olympic Games and which are particularly obvious in the excellent organization of the festival will constitute a permanent monument to the contribution which she has made to human culture in general. All those who appreciate the symbolism of the sacred flame which has been borne from Olympia to Berlin are profoundly grateful to your Excellency for having not only provided the means of binding

Spirydon Louis, winner of the 1896 Olympic marathon, leads the Greek team to a wreath-laying ceremony at a war memorial on the morning of the opening ceremony. (*Author's collection*)

the past and the present, but also for having contributed to the progress of the Olympic ideals in future years.

Hitler thanked the IOC for giving Germany 'the opportunity of furthering the eternal Olympic ideals'. He ended by announcing that the Greek Government had agreed to his suggestion that the excavations at ancient Olympia, carried out between 1875 and 1881 under the direction of German scholars, should be resumed, again under German supervision:

A sacred centre of ancient culture will thus be made available to present-day humanity. I hope that this work will assist in preserving the memories of the Olympic Games of 1936 throughout the future years. That unqualified success may attend the Berlin Festival is my sincere wish and that of the entire German nation.

As the IOC president and the German Chancellor were indulging in this display of mutual admiration, the saluting company of the

23rd Artillery Regiment was arriving at the Reich Sports Field. Then the first of 170 motor-coaches arranged by the army began unloading athletes brought from the Olympic Village. In bus number 150 was the Indian contingent, their golden kullahs set in light-blue turbans. The Indians arrived at the Bell Tower at 2.15 p.m. and marched to the May Field where the national teams had been divided into two groups, on the north and south sides, facing each other. India was on the south, Italy on her right and Haiti, which was represented by only one athlete, on her left. Holland was facing India, with Great Britain and Iceland on either side. In front of each team stood a student from the German National Socialist Educational Institution, holding a board which bore that team's name; behind the board holder stood the national flag bearer.

The stadium gates had been opened at 1.00 p.m. and the 78,054 paying ticket holders were soon in their places. With 8,617 complimentary tickets, 3,637 competitors and support staff, and 1,051 newspaper, radio and film journalists and technicians, the actual attendance was officially registered at 91,359, some way short of the 100,000 generally quoted over the years. But whatever their number, spectators were well entertained while they waited. The Olympic Symphony Orchestra, formed from the Berlin Philharmonic Orchestra and the National Orchestra, with other reinforcements, presented a concert under the direction of Professor Gustav Havemann of the Berlin Music Academy. Then the biggest airship in the world, the *Hindenburg*, which nine months later would meet its tragic end in New Jersey, cruised over the stadium. It flew slowly over the arena, the five Olympic rings and the inscription 'XI Olympiade Berlin 1936' painted on its silver sides, a huge Olympic flag fluttering from its gondola. On its tail-fins, however, there were stark reminders of these Games' over-tones: swastika emblems in black, red and white. The official report commented: 'It greeted the thousands assembled for the Olympic Games as the symbol of German inventive genius and workmanship.'

Far below *Hindenburg*, gymnastic demonstration teams quartered at Döberitz and Elsgrund barracks were also making their way to the Olympic Stadium; they were transported by train to Pichelsberg Station before being marched through the Equestrian Gate and tunnel to the sunken passageway around the arena. Members of the students' and youth encampments arrived after having been taken in motor-coaches from the Lustgarten to their camps for lunch.

Adolf Hitler's motorcade comes through the Brandenburg Gate. (*Author's collection*)

They were assigned standing room in the middle and upper galleries of the stadium.

At 3.00 p.m., a cavalcade of heavy, black Mercedes-Benzes swept out of the Reich Chancellery: first government ministers; then IOC members; and finally, the Führer himself, dressed in brown military uniform, wearing the Iron Cross, and standing upright in the open-top car next to his driver. Hitler's left hand, encased in a kid glove, rested upon the top of the windscreen, his right arm returning – in a peculiar limp manner – the Nazi salutes from the crowd as the procession made its way from Wilhemstrasse along the Via Triumphalis. To cries of 'Heil!' it swept through the Brandenburg Gate, from which hung yet more huge swastika and Olympic banners, and into Unter den Linden. The streets were lined with the military, including members of the National Socialist Motor Corps, stormtroopers and special National Socialist guards who kept back the thousands packing the pavements. More fortunate onlookers had gained vantage points from windows along the route, and waved flags and handkerchiefs. As the procession passed by, a wave of applause swelled from each section of the crowd. And always there were the Nazi salutes flung skywards

At the Reich Sports Field, cars carrying government ministers took them straight to the stadium and their boxes. The German Chancellor, together with members of the IOC and the Organizing Committee were driven on to the Bell Tower. There, the Olympic officials formed up ready to greet Hitler on the huge May Field, where an honour guard representing all three military services was drawn up, together with every athlete taking part in the Games. When Hitler's car arrived at 3.50 p.m., the light rain which had glistened on roads and pavements, and dampened the clothes, if not the spirits, of spectators, athletes and officials alike, suddenly stopped. As if by command, chinks of blue sky began to appear.

At the precise moment Hitler stepped on to the huge arena, the *Olympic Fanfare* composed by Paul Winter rang out from the two towers of the Marathon Gate. Accompanied by the Reich Minister of Defence, Werner von Blomberg, the Führer reviewed the military honour guard before being greeted by IOC and

Hitler walks through the May Field, accompanied by IOC members.
(*Author's collection*)

Organizing Committee members who then fell into place behind him. With Count Baillet-Latour on his right, and Theodor Lewald on his left, the German Chancellor crossed the May Field between the ranks of assembled athletes and, as the clock struck 4.00 p.m., entered the stadium and descended the Marathon Steps. Hitler's arrival was met by another fanfare, and a huge roar from the crowd, so huge in fact that those present swore they felt the very foundations of the new stadium sway beneath them. As tens of thousands of spectators rose from their seats, the music of *Huldigungsmarsch* (Homage March) by Richard Wagner fought to be heard over the noise of the crowd.

The Führer strode along the red running track with his entourage to the centre of the arena, where he was met by a small girl in a pretty blue dress; Gudrum Diem, the 5-year-old daughter of

The Führer strides into the Olympic Stadium. (*Author's collection*)

the secretary-general, bent a knee and greeted Hitler with 'Heil, mein Führer', before presenting him with a bouquet of flowers 'for which he expressed his hearty thanks'. Following the rendition of an introductory theme composed by Herbert Windt – who had collaborated with film-maker Leni Riefenstahl to produce a film of the huge 1934 Nazi Party rally in Nuremburg – Hitler climbed the steps to what was effectively a 'royal box' and took his place of honour. To his right was Count Baillet-Latour wearing a sombre morning coat left open to display his Olympic regalia, then Reich Minister Frick, Rudolf Hess, the deputy Führer, and Field Marshall von Blomberg, like Hitler all wearing military uniform. To the Führer's left was Umberto, the Crown Prince of Italy, then Theodor Lewald, both in civilian dress, and to their left Goebbels and Göring, again resplendent in uniform. Beside Göring, Leni Riefenstahl directed the movements of a bulky film camera.

As Hitler raised his arm to greet the sea of people, the German national anthem was played, and then there were spontaneous choruses of the 'Horst Wessel Song'. Naval personnel began to hoist the flags of fifty nations to the tops of masts set right around the stadium. Then all eyes turned to the west as the great Olympic Bell began to ring out, softly at first but increasing until it boomed around the stadium, calling upon the youth of the world.

The Berlin Olympics were filmed by Leni Riefenstahl for her *Olympia* films and also by Telefunken, to be relayed by television. (*Author's collection*)

It was now the turn of the teams to enter the arena. First came the placard bearer, then, 15 ft behind, the flag bearer; there were 20 yards between each team. In they came, marching two, three, four, five and six abreast depending on their number. The blue and white flag of Greece, home of the first modern Olympiad, led the way; it was carried by a sprightly 60-year-old, Spirydon Louis, winner of the 1896 Olympic marathon. The rest came in alphabetical order, although Egypt, wearing red fezes, led the way because the German name for their country begins with the letter 'A'. Again taking into account the German spelling, the Egyptians were followed by Afghanistan, Argentina, Australia, Belgium, Bermuda, Bolivia, Brazil, Bulgaria, Chile, China, Colombia, Costa Rica, Denmark, Estonia, Finland, France, Great Britain, Haiti, Holland, India, Iceland, Italy, Japan, Yugoslavia, Canada, Latvia, Liechtenstein, Luxembourg, Malta, Mexico, Monaco, New Zealand, Norway, Austria, Peru, Philippine Islands, Poland, Portugal, Rumania, Sweden, Switzerland, South Africa, Czechoslovakia, Turkey, Hungary, Uruguay, USA, and finally, the hosts, Germany. Missing from the original entrants were Jamaica, Panama and Spain.

The teams marched the length of the stadium along the running track, dipping their flags as they passed Hitler and the other guests of honour. Some gave the Nazi salute; some did not. The British team, led by the veteran Jack Beresford, the most accomplished oarsman in Olympic history before Sir Steven Redgrave, favoured a smart eyes-right; like that of the Americans at Garmisch-Partenkirchen, this drew only polite applause. Perhaps thinking back to that moment, the USA team, dressed in blue blazers and white trousers, whipped off their straw hats and clapped them over their hearts, a gesture that did not go down much better than their previous one. The Italians inevitably gave the fascist salute, and were rewarded with hearty applause. The Bulgarians joined in with a goose step. Whatever the teams did, everyone on the platform – with the exception of the Belgian Baillet-Latour, and Riefenstahl, who was busy telling her cameraman what to do – returned the Nazi salute.

Finally, to the heavy beat of Frederick the Great's stirring *Hohenfriedberger March*, the German team entered the stadium. Dressed in all-white naval-style uniforms, including yachting caps, they were greeted by a roar that rivalled even that which had welcomed the Führer himself. Every German in the stadium – which was practically everyone there – rose to their feet, right arms raised in the Nazi salute. At the northern side of the running track, all the teams turned left and formed rows, presenting a magnificent picture against the green background of the field.

Despite the modest receptions accorded to the British and Americans, overall the whole procession had been well-received. A Swedish journalist wrote: 'I believed that the walls would burst. Had there been a roof over the stadium it would certainly have been blown away, since the entire bowl was a cauldron of stormy enthusiasm.'

A Parisian correspondent declared:

At the reception accorded the French team, one had the feeling that a great moment had arrived in the history of the world. Never was the war threat on the Rhine less than during these moments. Never were the French more popular in Germany than on this occasion. It was a demonstration, but one of comradeship and the will for peace.

A Danish journalist supplied a more personal note:

It is a pity that Baron de Coubertin was not present. What a pleasure it would have been for him to see his great ideal realized in so magnificent and worthy a fashion in the gigantic, newly constructed Colosseum of Berlin.

The Dane's sentiments were shared by many, and a bronze relief of de Coubertin created by the Frankfurt sculptor, Richard Werner, was later unveiled in the IOC's meeting room.

Yet although he could not be present in person, the voice of de Coubertin now echoed around the stadium. The 73-year-old had recorded his message on a gramophone disc. In French, he reminded the huge crowd: 'The important thing in the Olympic Games is not winning but taking part; the essential thing in life is not conquering but fighting well.' His words appeared in translation on the stadium announcement board. Then Theodor Lewald stepped up to speak. Lewald droned on for 15 minutes, but British radio listeners were left in ignorance as the BBC commentator, Tommy Woodroofe, soon gave up trying to understand what the president of the Organizing Committee was telling his huge audience. Instead, Woodroofe, in his plummy voice, complained that the speech was far too long, and then began to fill in by mentioning the weather, the *Hindenburg* and anything else that caught his fancy; in particular, he seemed obsessed by the fact that the grass was green. Woodroofe's concentration eventually lapsed to the point where he missed entirely the moment that Lewald stepped aside and Hitler came forward to open the Games. (The following year, Woodroofe began a drunken account of the Spithead Naval Review in which he rambled on for four minutes about 'fairylights' before the BBC filled in with thirty minutes of unscheduled dance music.)

After Lewald's long-winded address, Hitler was brief: 'I proclaim open the Olympic Games of Berlin, celebrating the eleventh Olympiad of the modern era.' Then the remaining members of the IOC and Organizing Committee entered the arena and formed to the right and left of the speakers' platform. The commander of the procession, Major Edgar Feuchtinger, gave the command 'Hoist flag' and the Olympic emblem was raised slowly to the top of its mast at the west end of the stadium. The artillery detachment fired saluting salvos, and clouds of carrier pigeons arose from the walls of the May Field. Each one bore the colours of the competing nations, and carried news of the opening of the Games. Trumpets were again heard from the towers at the Marathon Gate, this time playing the opening fanfare of Richard Strauss's *Olympic Hymn* which was being given its first public airing. Strauss himself, dressed in a white coat, conducted his composition, and the stadium resounded to the sound of a huge choir.

Strauss's involvement in the 1936 Olympics is interesting. In November 1933, without any consultation with the composer, Goebbels appointed him president of the Reichsmusikkammer, the Reich Chamber of Music which sought not only to promote musicians but also to control their music. Strauss decided to accept the post but to remain apolitical, a naïve decision perhaps, but apparently one intended to protect his Jewish daughter-in-law. In 1935, however, Strauss was forced to resign his position after refusing to remove from the playbill for his opera *Die Schweigsame Frau* the name of a Jewish librettist, Stefan Zweig. He had written Zweig a supportive letter, criticizing the Nazis, which was intercepted by the Gestapo. Strauss was forbidden from appearing in public for a year, but he was such a well-known figure that the Nazis probably felt that allowing him to compose the *Olympic Hymn* would be a positive signal to the rest of the world.

At the same moment that Hitler's cavalcade had left the Chancellery, the last torch relay runners had set off from the Lustgarten. Their route had been precisely mapped out: Unter den Linden, the Brandenburg Gate, Hindenburg Platz, Charlottenburger Chaussee, Bismarck Strasse, Kaiserdamm, Adolf Hitler Platz (the last great square before the stadium), Reichs Strasse, Olympische

Fritz Schilgen, a German 1500m runner, caries the torch on the last lap of its 3000km journey.
(*Author's collection*)

Strasse, Olympischer Platz (north traffic lane), Olympic Gate, then the eastern entrance to the Olympic Stadium, the eastern steps, the southern running track to the western gate. Now, as the last strains of Strauss's composition died away, cheers were heard outside the stadium as the final torch bearer, Fritz Schilgen, a German 1500 m runner, came into sight. An archetypal flaxen-haired 'Aryan', Schilgen appeared in the gap at the top of the steps, pausing for a moment as the crowd gasped and then fell silent. Then he began his descent into the arena, running lightly down the eastern steps. Trotting anti-clockwise around the track, he passed the massed ranks of the teams formed up on the field, then with strong strides climbed the Marathon Steps. After holding the torch aloft for a final time, Schilgen reached up to ignite the fuel in the giant bronze altar. As the fire burst into life and the flame shot skywards, another huge roar shook the stadium. (Fritz Schilgen died on 12 September 2005, four days after his ninety-ninth birthday.)

There were two further ceremonies to complete. First, the 1896 marathon victor, Spirydon Louis, mounted the steps to the box where Hitler stood, and presented the German Chancellor with an olive branch from Olympia. Then national flag-bearers formed a semi-circle around the speakers' platform. Accompanying the German flag-bearer was Rudolf Ismayr, who had won a weightlifting gold for Germany in the 1932 Games. The flags were dipped, and while all participants raised their right hand, Ismayr, a large swastika flag at his left hand, took the Olympic Oath on their behalf:

> We swear that we will take part in the Olympic Games in loyal competition, respecting the regulations which govern them, and desirous of participating in them in the true spirit of sportsmanship for the honour of our country and for the glory of sport.

Handel's *Hallelujah Chorus*, sung by the 3,000-strong choir, followed the oath. At 5.45 p.m., the teams began to leave the stadium, again marching past Hitler before passing through the Marathon Gate. When the last athlete had disappeared, the Führer took leave of the presidents of the IOC and Organizing Committee and departed to Paul Winter's concluding fanfare, trumpeted once more from the towers. That evening, a festival entitled 'Olympic Youth' was held in the stadium. Organized by Carl Diem and arranged and directed by Hans Niedecken-Gebhard, the festival saw thousands of children pouring into the stadium down the

The white-uniformed German team bring up the rear of the procession of competing nations. (*Author's collection*)

On the evening of the opening ceremony the Olympic Stadium staged a spectacular youth festival. (*Author's collection*)

Marathon Steps. There was music, singing, and dancing, and games on the green central arena, all set off by brilliant floodlighting. Everyone agreed that it had been a joyous experience.

Besides that to be held in the stadium, there would be two more flame-lighting ceremonies at the 1936 Summer Games. Relay runners took the Olympic fire 215 miles from Berlin to Kiel, where the yachting competition was to be held, and twenty miles (it should have been less but a zig-zag route was devised to eke it out) to Grünau, site of the canoeing and rowing events.

Over the next sixteen days, visitors arrived day and night at Berlin's railway stations and airports, while the autobahns leading to the city were filled with thousands of vehicles. The official lodgings bureau worked tirelessly, as, according to the police registration, more than 1.2 million guests arrived in Berlin during the period of the Olympic Games, 150,000 of them foreigners. On 9 August alone, 160,000 people arrived by train; a departure record was set on 16 August when 200,000 passed through the railway stations at the Games' end. The Reichsbank alone transacted business to the extent of 23 million Reichsmarks through the Olympic Foreign Exchange Bureau. What shocked the foreign visitors was the military nature of everything, and the hysteria that greeted Hitler wherever he went. Of course, there was also some sport.

Chapter Ten

A FLYING START

In early August 1936, the prairie states of the USA were suffering yet again from the fierce heat and drought that earned the region its 'Dust Bowl' label throughout the 1930s. In Berlin, however, American athletes had been complaining about the cold as overcast skies, light rain and an unseasonably cool wind had done their best to spoil the ceremonial opening of the Olympic Games. Gloomy skies persisted into the first day of competition, but overall conditions were a little better as the first events got under way on the Sunday morning of 2 August. The Olympic Stadium was again packed, this time for the first heats in the track and field athletics. The huge crowd – the stadium averaged 81,835 paying spectators for each of the eight days' athletics held there – particularly wanted to see that most explosive of Olympic events: the men's 100 m.

German hopes were pinned on their giant sprinter Eric Borchmeyer, a member of the 4 × 100 m relay team that had won silver at Los Angeles in 1932. Just before those Games, Borchmeyer and his teammates had set a new world record of 40.6 seconds at Kassel for that event. The Dutch pair of Christiaan Berger and Martinus Osendarp were also fancied. Berger had equalled the world record of 10.3 seconds – which was also the current Olympic record – in Amsterdam two years earlier. Like Berger, Osendarp would eventually hold the European record at 100 m and 200 m. Moreover, he became so impressed with the Nazis' apparent promotion of sport that, when his country was occupied in 1940, he would serve as a police officer, joining the SS and the NSB, the Dutch National Socialist Party, for which actions he was imprisoned after the war.

But there was one athlete, above all others, who the crowd wanted to see. Jesse Owens, a 22-year-old African-American student from Ohio State University, had burst upon the world athletics stage during the Big Ten inter-college meeting at Ann Arbor, Michigan, on the afternoon of 25 May 1935. Owens had turned up not even sure if he would compete following a fall downstairs in which he had hurt his back; but in just 45 minutes that afternoon he broke three world records – 220 yds, 220 yds low hurdles and long jump – and equalled another in the 100 yds. Some credit Owens with setting five world records, saying he also beat the marks for the shorter 200 m and 200 m low hurdles. Five records or three, in the *New York Times*, columnist Arthur Daley called Owens's performances 'the greatest day in track history'. Then the IAAF confirmed that, in Chicago on 20 June 1936, Owens had broken the world record for the 100 m; his time of 10.2 seconds was not beaten for twenty years.

It was everything Owens had ever wanted. When he was a pupil at Fairmont Junior High School in Cleveland, his coach had brought to the school one Charley Paddock, an American sprinter famed for his 'flying finish', a kind of leaping lunge at the tape. Paddock had won the 100 m gold at the 1920 Antwerp Olympics; he became known as 'The World's Fastest Human Being' after setting a new world record of 10.4 seconds in April 1921, a time not equalled until 1929, and not beaten until a year after that. The young Owens was charged with lining up his classmates in orderly fashion to obtain the great sprinter's autograph, and was later invited into the coach's office to meet his idol. Paddock shook Owens by the hand and wished him well. Later, the coach asked Owens his opinion of Paddock. According to Owens, he replied: 'Well, gee, coach, I would sure like to be known as "The World's Fastest Human Being" someday.'

Despite attending a northern university, well away from the Deep South of his early childhood – the family had moved to Ohio when he was 9 – at college Owens had experienced plenty of bigotry against his own race in a country where segregation was enshrined in law. He lived in a house with other black members of the track team and took most of his meals there. Black team members could not always dine in restaurants or use restroom facilities when the team was travelling to or from meetings. In November 1935, shortly after the Nuremburg Laws were passed, persecuting all non-Aryans, Owens had spoken out publicly against going to the Berlin Games, but his coach, Larry Snyder, advised him against taking a position. Now, on this chilly day in Berlin, Owens had to concentrate on the task ahead.

Jesse – real name James Cleveland, but on his first day at a new school, a northern teacher heard 'Jesse' not 'J C' and that was what he would be called thereafter – was not running until the last of the twelve 100 m heats, which began at 10.30 a.m. The first two in each heat would go through to the second round. Besides the cloud cover, a 4½mph wind coming diagonally and from behind made the day feel cooler than the 64°F recorded when the first sprinters lined up. Berger won his heat in 10.8 seconds, Osendarp in 10.5, and

Jesse Owens was about to become a Olympic Games legend. (*Author's collection*)

Borchmeyer in 10.7. Starting blocks were not yet allowed in competitive races and the sprinters had to dig their own starting holes in the cinder track. For this they were provided with starting trowels in leather cases, on which were printed the words: 'XI Olympiade Berlin 1936.' The official report comments:

> The competitors were pleased with these souvenirs. The result however, was that other equipment was also looked upon as souvenirs. The judges who were responsible for the return of the equipment had difficulty in preventing the competitors from carrying off javelins, discuses, relay batons, etc.

Jesse Owens already had his eyes on the only souvenirs he wanted from these games: gold medals. Thanks to Leni Riefenstahl's iconic filmwork, we can still study his style: Owens was an unusual runner, for a world champion at any rate. He possessed a curious, low action in which he did not appear to raise his knees too much for the first 30 m. None of this really mattered, however, when it came to the twelfth heat of the 1936 men's 100 m first round. Owens simply raced against himself. He won with

Four of the fastest men in the world. From left to right: Frank Wykoff, Paul Hänni, Ralph Metcalfe and Jesse Owens. (*Author's collection*)

metres to spare, equalling the Olympic record of 10.3 seconds in the process. A measure of Owens's lead at the tape is the fact that the second man, Kichizo Sasaki of Japan, did not beat 11 seconds. The second round of heats began at 3.00 p.m. and this time Owens was drawn to run early on, in the second heat. Again, he stormed to the finish, this time in 10.2 seconds. The following wind had picked up a little and the official reports says that, but for this, Owens's time 'would have constituted a new world record', although the IAAF now recognizes that he had already set that record in Chicago six weeks earlier. This time Owens left the Swiss sprinter Paul Hänni trailing in his wake, five metres behind at 10.6, with Jozsef Sir of Hungary slipping into the third qualifying place.

Borchmeyer also won his heat, as did Owens's fellow African-American, Ralph Metcalfe, both in 10.5 seconds; Metcalfe had won silver at Los Angeles in 1932, behind another American, Thomas 'Eddie' Tolan. In the first heat, Osendarp had finished in second place behind the Swede, Lennart Strandberg, while Owens and Metcalfe were joined in the semi-finals by the white American schoolteacher, Frank Wykoff. Britain had two runners through: Oxford University's Alan Pennington, one of several

Eric Borchmeyer (right) chats to the Hungarian sprinter, Jozsef Sir. All Germany's hopes in the 100m were pinned on Borchmeyer. (*Author's collection*)

Achilles club members competing in Berlin, and Dublin-born Arthur Sweeney, the 1934 Empire Games gold medallist at 100 yds and 220 yds. But it was Jesse Owens who stood head and shoulders above everyone else, and anyone with tickets for the second day of competition must have been savouring the prospect of seeing him in action.

While the sprinters had stolen the show in that first day, there was plenty more fascinating action in the arena of the Olympic Stadium, not least the winning of the first gold medal of the 1936 Summer Games – and by a German too. Spot on 3.00 p.m., fourteen athletes, representing ten nations, came out for the first round of the women's javelin. After three attempts each, eight were eliminated including the 24-year-old Briton, Kathleen Connal, whose throw of 27.80 m was woefully short of the 35.99 m that had won her the AAA's championship title a few weeks earlier. In contrast, Germany's Tilly Fleischer, with her second throw of the first round, had passed the Olympic record of 43.68 m – set in 1932 by America's Mildred 'Babe' Didrikson – by a metre.

By the time the final round got under way, the sun had broken through and for the first time the packed Olympic Stadium looked something like the picture everyone had imagined for these Games. Luse Krüger of Germany led the way with 40.69 m; Fleischer, with only 38.87 m, trailed last of the six first-round survivors. With her second throw of the final, however, Fleischer put in a tremendous effort; her javelin soared through the air and even before the official distance could be measured and posted, there was a roar from the crowd who sensed that they had just seen history in the making. Sure enough, the German's throw had established a new Olympic record of 45.18 m (148 ft 2½ ins). The nearest anyone had got to her in that round was the 41.37 m achieved by her fellow German, Lydia Eberhardt. Fleischer could not improve upon her record in the final round of throws – indeed, Krüger's 42.96 m just edged her – but the gold medal was hers. Krüger took silver with her 43.29 m from the first round, and the bronze went to the Pole, Maria Kwasniewska, whose very first throw of the competition had gone 41.80 m. No one, however, had got near the American Nan Grindele's world record 46.74 m set in Chicago in 1932. The one surprise of the event had been the performance of the European champion, Herma Bauma of Austria, who had been one of the favourites; Bauma's best throw was 41.66 m, although at the London Olympics of 1948 she would take gold with 45.57 m.

Fleischer was mobbed and cheered wherever she went. Spectators hanging over the high wall surrounding the area

Tilly Fleischer was mobbed wherever she went after winning gold for Germany with a new Olympic record in the javelin.
(*Author's collection*)

yelled for her to come over and sign autograph books, programmes and any other bits of paper they could find. They clapped their hands, stamped their feet, chanted her name. Even the Führer himself would have been delighted with such a reception. In fact, Hitler had not been present to witness these early German triumphs, but he arrived back at the stadium just before 5.30 p.m., when the semi-final of the shot put was about to begin. Although the elimination competition had been held in the cooler morning, the arrival of the late afternoon sun had pushed the temperature up to a pleasant 68°F as Germany's hopes – Hans Wöllke, a 25-year-old Berlin policeman, and Gerhard Stöck from the Charlottenburg club in Berlin – prepared to do battle with the giant 22-stone-American, Jack Torrance, who in Oslo in 1934 had posted a world record of 17.40 m (57 ft). In Torrance's huge grasp the shot looked like a tennis ball, but it was Sulo Bärlund of Finland who set the standard in Berlin by establishing a new Olympic record of 16.03 m with his second attempt. It was a short-lived triumph: Wöllke, whose best effort in the semi-finals had been 15.96 m, put in a mighty effort with his second put of the final; as with Fleischer's record-breaking javelin throw, so the crowd knew that Wöllke had bested the best. The announcement that he had achieved 16.20 m was greeted by yet another huge roar. As Bärlund tried to wrest back the lead there was a breathless hush – and then some worried Germans when they saw his shot sail past the 16 m mark. But it went only 12 cm past and the final round had produced nothing to change the order. Stöck led that with 15.66 m, while Wöllke had used up his one great effort and recorded only 14.98 m with his final attempt. Again, Germany had gold – and this time bronze, for Stöck – while Bärlund took silver. Rumours coming out of the Olympic Village that Torrance was out of condition had proved well-founded and the American finished fifth, his best effort almost a metre behind that of the winner.

Hans Wöllke, whose mighty effort in the shot won another gold for Germany. (*Author's collection*)

These early German triumphs put Hitler in a remarkably good mood and that evening he received the Germans Wöllke and Stöck, and Fleischer and Krüger, in his box, along with Kwasniewska and Bärlund, and three other Finns – Ilmari Salminen, Arvo Askola and Volmari Iso-Hollo, gold, silver and bronze medallists respectively in the 10,000 m that had also started at 5.30 p.m. For a long time, the Japanese runner, Kohei Murakoso, had maintained the lead in that race, but 500 m from the finish he could only watch as all three Finns swept past him. Salminen's time of 30 minutes 15.4 seconds was four seconds outside the Olympic record. Britain's only representative, Alex Burns of Elswick Harriers, came fifth. After Burns died at the

Ilmari Salminen and Volmari Iso-Hollo, gold and bronze medals respectively in the 10,000 m. Fellow countryman Arvo Askola finished second to make it a clean sweep for Finland. (*Author's collection*)

age of 95 in May 2003, a plaque was unveiled in his honour on his native Tyneside, but in August 1936 he was 38 seconds too late at the finishing line to be invited to meet the Führer of Germany.

After receiving the Finns, who had run a brilliant tactical team race, Hitler left the stadium before the result of the men's high jump was announced. He would have known that the result would be a blow to his notion of Aryan supremacy. During the United States final Olympic trials held in New York in July, both Cornelius Johnson and Dave Albritton had set a world record – not officially ratified until after the Games – of 2.07 m (6 ft 9 ins). Not only were both American, they were both black. Johnson approached the Olympic final with almost contemptuous ease, not even bothering to remove his tracksuit until the final jump-off. He took the gold with a jump of 2.03 m, easily beating the old record of 1.98 m set back in 1924 in Paris. Despite being troubled by an ankle injury,

Cornelius Johnson won the high jump although he failed to improve upon his world record. (*Author's collection*)

Albritton won silver, and the white American, Delos Thurber, took the bronze, although places two-to-four were decided by a jump-off with Finland's European champion, Kalevi Kotkas, finishing just outside the medals. Not satisfied with just an Olympic record, Johnson pushed on for the world mark, still officially American Walter Marty's 2.06 m at Palo Alto in April 1934. Having already cleared 2.07 m in his country's Olympic trials, Johnson had the bar set at 2.08 m but, three times in the gathering dusk, he failed to clear it. He would not have long to wait, however, for his, and Albritton's feat, to be recognized.

For Britain it had been a day of mixed fortunes. Burns had given his best in the 10,000 m, while Pennington and Sweeney had won through to the 100 m semi-finals. In the 800 m, the British team was sorely missing the Scot, James 'Hamish' Stothard, who had won the 880 yds bronze in the 1934 Empire Games. The following year, Stothard, a student at Cambridge, had taken the 800 m gold at the International Universities Championships in Budapest, but had struggled to find his form in the run-up to the Olympics, during which he had suffered with injury (in his old age he finished up with two titanium knees). Through in their heats of the 800 m were John Powell, Frank Handley and Brian McCabe, but in the high jump, shot put and women's javelin, British hopes had been already dashed.

For some, of course, Olympic success did lie ahead. Godfrey Brown, a 21-year-old Cambridge University student who had been born in Bengal, was a highly talented and versatile runner at any distance from 100 yds to the half-mile. He went to Berlin as the AAA's 440 yds champion and was entered in the 400 m and the 4 × 400 m relay. Brown came from a sporting family: sister Audrey was in Britain's 4 × 400 m relay team for these Olympics; brother Ralph had won the AAA's 440 yds hurdles title in 1934.

That Brown was a student was typical of the British team, who were drawn from either universities, the armed forces or everyday jobs in civvy street. Those in the military at least had some time to practise, although very little compared to the status of some competitors – Germans in particular – who were, to all intents and purposes, full-time athletes. The British team captain, Don Finlay, who was in the RAF, eventually enjoyed a highly distinguished twenty-year career as an international athlete, from his debut in the long jump, against France in 1929 to his victory, again against France, in the 120 yds hurdles in 1949, when he clocked a new British record. At the 1932 Los Angeles Olympics, Finlay had split the Americans in the 110 m hurdles to take bronze. He came to

Berlin as the Empire Games sprint hurdles champion and, like Godfrey and Audrey Brown, would find Olympic success there.

That evening it was announced that the gold medal in the buildings section of the Olympic art competition had gone to Werner and Walter March for the Reich Sports Field, ahead of Charles Downing Lay's Marine Park in Brooklyn. The Marches' entry also won silver in the architectural section, behind the Austrian architect Hermann Kutschera's design for a skiing stadium. There were also competitions for painting and graphic art, literature, sculpture and music. The merits of buildings, pictures, statues, musical compositions and the written word were, however, far from the minds of athletes who slept fitfully in the Olympic Village, wondering instead what the second day of sporting competition might bring.

Chapter Eleven

MYTH AND REALITY

The 85,000 people who flooded into the Olympic Stadium on Monday, 3 August 1936 had only one focus: the final of the men's 100 m. They had a fairly long wait too, because even the semi-finals were not scheduled to start until 3.30 p.m. Until then, spectators in the stadium itself would have to make do with the early stages of the hammer competition, although those with tickets for other venues could watch Great Britain beat Mexico 13–11 at polo on the May Field; freestyle wrestling in the Hall of German Sport – where among British hopes, featherweight Norman Morrell defeated the German Bock (later in the day Morrell was eliminated by Francis Millard of the USA who went on to win the silver medal); or the epée section of the modern pentathlon in the Cupola Hall of the Hall of German Sport.

It was, however, the track that had most people's attention. The first events there started at 3.00 p.m. with the heats of the men's 400 m hurdles. These produced no surprises with America's Glenn Hardin – everyone's fancy for the gold medal – going through to the semi-finals. Two years earlier, running in Stockholm, Hardin had knocked a full second off the existing world record and his time on that occasion, 50.6 seconds, would not be beaten for nineteen years. On this damp, overcast day in Berlin, he was slow – 53.9 seconds – but besides the atmosphere which was hardly conducive to making muscles supple, there was also a diagonal wind, first helping, then hindering the runners. In Hardin's heat, Britain's only hope, John Sheffield, the AAA's 440 yds hurdles champion, finished last and was eliminated. In the semi-final, Hardin improved slightly to win in 53.2 seconds. Before he could line up for the final, however, the 100 m semi-finals were scheduled. The first three in each of the two heats would go through to the final, due to take place at 5.00 p.m. that afternoon, and this time Owens was drawn in the first heat, and in the outside lane. He went about one-third of the way before raising his upper body. Then, staring intently down the track at the finishing tape, he left teammate Frank Wykoff and Sweden's Lennart Strandberg trailing to win in 10.4, a full one-tenth of a second ahead of them. It seemed utterly effortless and he would surely have at least equalled his own Olympic record but for the damp track. As Wykoff and Strandberg strained towards the tape, Owens was almost leaning back, looking more a man who had just jogged home in a middle-distance race. After he had crossed the line, his speed of deceleration was almost as amazing as his forward thrust; he came to a standstill while all the other runners shot past him. In the second heat, the times were again slower than would normally have been expected from world-class sprinters. Ralph Metcalfe won in 10.5 seconds, followed by Osendarp and Borchmeyer. British hopes had, as expected, died at this stage: Pennington finished last in Owens's heat; Sweeney fifth in Metcalfe's. In their disappointment they joined Powell and Handley, both of whom had failed to join their fellow Briton, Brian McCabe, in the 800 m final. Britain's Tommy Evenson and Jim Ginty had also been eliminated in the heats of the 3000 m steeplechase.

Jesse Owens now had to keep in shape. The cheers he received from the huge crowd would have warmed the cockles of anyone's heart, but the champion-elect was more concerned about his legs. He pulled on his tracksuit, then found a large blanket and went to chat to his teammates. Before he raced again, however, came the final of the hammer. Britain's only representative, Norman Drake, had gone out almost immediately, failing to throw

Jesse Owens wins the 100m ahead of Metcalfe and Osendarp. (*Author's collection*)

Karl Hein's winning hammer throw of 56.49 m would stand as an Olympic record until 1952.
(*Author's collection*)

the required 46 m. The competition soon developed into a straight contest between two Germans – a Hamburg carpenter called Karl Hein, and Erwin Blask of the Berliner SC – and the Swede, Fred Warngård. Blask went through to the final with a throw of 55.04 m, a new Olympic record breaking the 54.74 m set by America's Matthew McGrath back in 1912 in Stockholm. Warngård (54.03 m) and Hein (52.44 m) joined him, although Hein, in third place, looked nervous. Yet in the final – to the accompaniment of a mighty chant 'Hein! Hein! Hein!' – he produced three magnificent efforts: 54.7 m; then a new Olympic record of 54.85 m; and finally a stunning 56.49 m (185 ft 4 ins) which would stand until 1952. Blask took the silver, Warngård the bronze. In the VIP box, the Nazi leaders were beside themselves: The smile on Hitler's face developed into a huge grin of Cheshire Cat-like proportions; Göring bounced up and down in his seat like a child. In almost anyone else it would have been a picture of unbridled, innocent joy.

One man who watched the hammer final with mixed emotions was Dr Pat O'Callaghan, who had won gold at the previous two Olympics. After Irish independence in 1922, the National Athletic and Cycling Association of Ireland (NACAI) maintained its jurisdiction over all of Ireland including the partitioned six counties of Ulster. The British AAA, however, laid claim to Ulster's athletes. After the 1932 Olympics, the AAA and the British Olympic Committee intensified their claim and the controversy came to a head when the IAAF finally disqualified the NACAI. Thus, no Irish team travelled to the 1936 Olympics, and O'Callaghan, a staunch defender of the idea of a united Ireland, closed his last door to international competition. Instead he travelled to Berlin as a private spectator and watched the Games from the VIP seats, attended IOC banquets and was presented to Baillet-Latour and other senior IOC officials as well as to Hitler himself.

At this latest German triumph, Hitler was entertaining in his box the Jew-hating Julius Streicher, and the boxer Max Schmeling, a liberal German who had employed a Jewish manager. In November 1938, when Nazi pogroms against the Jews reached new depths, Schmeling agreed to hide the two teenage sons of a Jewish friend of his, and later helped them flee the country. For now, though, he was as delighted as his Führer when Germany again took the gold medal.

Before the 100 m final, there was one last drama to be played out, in the heats of the women's 100 m. The Polish girl, Stanislawa Walasiewiczówna, had grown up in Cleveland where she was known as Stella Walsh. She had been a gold medal prospect for the 1932 Olympics, but shortly before she was due to complete American naturalization, the department where she worked at the New Central Railroad of Cleveland was closed down and Walasiewiczówna accepted a job at the Polish consulate in New York, deciding to compete for the country of her birth instead. Running with what the Canadian official report described as 'long man-like strides', she equalled the world record in every one of her three races to take the gold in Los Angeles. In Berlin, Walasiewiczówna won her heat as expected, but all eyes were now on a 6ft-tall farm girl from Calloway County, Missouri. In 1935, Helen Stephens had set a new world record of 11.5 seconds, well ahead of Walasiewiczówna's Olympic record of 11.9 seconds; Walasiewiczówna won her own heat in 12.5 seconds. Like Owens, Stephens was a natural athlete. In her first-round heat she lived up to her reputation as the new sensation of women athletics, winning in 11.4 seconds, which would have been a new world and Olympic record but for a gentle following wind. As she breasted the tape she was a good 10 m ahead of her nearest rival, Mildred Dolson of

The world's fastest man and woman: Jesse Owens and America's female sprinting sensation, Helen Stephens. (*Author's collection*)

Canada. Late in the afternoon, Stephens would win again, this time in 11.5 seconds, again disallowed as a record. The following day she would blaze her way to gold with another wind-assisted 11.5; Walasiewiczówna would take silver in 11.7 seconds. The Polish girl, who was eventually granted American citizenship after the Second World War, died in 1980, the victim of a stray bullet fired by a shopping mall thief. The autopsy revealed that Walasiewiczówna was neither distinctly male nor female but had non-functioning male sex organs, and both male and female chromosomes, a condition known as mosaicism. In 1932, the Canadians had been more perceptive than perhaps they had realized.

All three British girls – Eileen Hiscock, Barbara Burke and Audrey Brown – would be spectators in the 1936 women's 100 m final. In the mean time, Stephens's stunning performance in the first round had set the stage perfectly for the entrance of the men's finalists, or more particularly that of Jesse Owens. Their moment arrived and at just before 5.00 p.m., the stadium hummed with expectation. Six men jogged up and down, limbering up around Herr Miller, the starter who was dressed all in white and sporting a .380 calibre pistol. Owens had been drawn in the inside lane; then the four white sprinters: Strandberg of Sweden; Borchmeyer of Germany; Osendarp of Holland; Wykoff of the United States; and Metcalfe in the outside lane. The runners dug their starting holes and then stared down the track at their target. The 100 m is about sheer physical power, but also about concentration and focus. Owens looked the calmest but, many years later, admitted to the *Saturday Evening Post*:

> I began to think in terms of what it had taken me to get there, the number of people who had counselled and coached me; and the people who believed in me – the community from which I had come and the school I attended ... I felt suddenly as if my legs could not carry even the weight of my body. My stomach said that it wasn't there. My mouth was as dry as cotton; the palms of my hands wet with perspiration.

The spectators had been momentarily distracted by a victory ceremony in the middle of the arena, where Karl Hein was receiving his gold medal for the hammer throw. As the German national anthem was taken up by the crowd, Owens's gaze drifted from the centre of the arena, across the vivid green grass to the red track with its brilliant white lines. Then he caught sight of the flags of every competing nation stirring lazily against their poles.

Suddenly, the starter's whistle brought every runner from his private thoughts and back to the job in hand. Owens stared down fixedly at the track under him, then wriggled his fingers before setting himself in his crouch. The stadium fell silent, muscles strained, Herr Miller's pistol cracked out and the runners exploded off the starting line together. At 30 m they were still together, but then Owens drew away, the race already decided in his favour. At 70 m Metcalfe broke free of the rest and advanced on Owens, but without ever threatening his chances of victory. Osendarp forged ahead of Wykoff to take the bronze. Strandberg pulled a ligament at the 50 m mark, leaving fifth place to Borchmeyer. Owens's time was 10.3 seconds, again equalling the Olympic record. The crowd, having long given up all hope that the German Borchmeyer would win gold, once they had seen Owens in action earlier in the competition, now generously applauded the African-American. Then came the incident that is still debated seventy years later.

Even today, mention of the 1936 Berlin Olympics almost inevitably draws forth the response: 'Oh, that was the one where Hitler refused to shake hands with Jesse Owens.' Yet for decades it has been widely acknowledged that this did not happen; at least, Hitler did not actually refuse to shake hands with the African-American son of a sharecropper from the Deep South. The story is far from straightforward. Twenty-four hours before Owens won his first gold, Hitler had received that day's medal winners in his box: Wöllke, Stöck, Fleischer, Krüger, Kwasniewska, Bärlund, Salminen, Askola, Iso-Hollo – they could all be described as Aryans, no Jewish, black or gypsy blood in sight according to the Nazis' warped theories.

Like everything else at these Olympics, the medal award ceremonies were planned down to the last detail. In the stadium arena, opposite the box which housed the guests of honour, a platform with three levels had been set up. Led by the white-uniformed young women of the Olympic Honorary Service, the victors ascended this platform for the announcement of the *Cérémonie protocolaire Olympique*. The gold medallist stood on the middle level, which was the highest. Right and left of him stood those who had taken silver and bronze. Young girls placed wreaths of oak leaves upon the heads of the medallists, who were each eventually also presented with a diploma and a small oak tree with the inscription: 'Grow in honour of victory, inspire to further achievements.'

On the second evening of the track and field events, Karl Hein was the first to receive his gold. As the swastika flag was run up the tallest of three flagpoles, and the German national anthem was blasted out across the stadium, Hein stood erect and gave Hitler the Nazi salute. The Führer returned the salute, and so did the 80,000-odd Germans in the crowd. It was a remarkable display of homage. Then Jesse Owens stepped up to receive his medal. The victor of the 100 m first bowed his head to receive his wreath of oak leaves, then straightened up as the band played 'The Star-Spangled Banner'. After the anthem, Owens bowed his head towards the VIP box, where Hitler acknowledged the gesture with a straight-armed salute before turning away.

The myth that Hitler had snubbed Owens by refusing to shake his hand is just that, but it is a legend born out of many varied accounts of what happened and what was said during those first two days of competition. The previous day, having received the white medallists in the hammer, 10,000 m and women's javelin, Hitler had left just before the American

Hitler, with Theodor Lewald on his right, salutes the athletes. The German Führer's 'snubbing' of Jesse Owens became the great myth of the Berlin Olympics. (*Author's collection*)

national anthem that heralded the high-jump gold medallist, and Owens's African-American teammate, Cornelius Johnson. Some contemporary accounts have Hitler 'storming out' of the stadium, or 'leaving the stadium in a tantrum'. There are, however, claims that he was planning to leave anyway; it was getting dark, starting to rain, and conditions for the kind of photo opportunities that he had taken with Wöllke and Fleischer had receded. Another explanation was that Hitler's party always entered and left the stadium on an exact prearranged schedule. Whatever the truth of the matter, if anyone had been snubbed, it could be said that it was Johnson and his colleague, Dave Albritton, who had taken the silver, and not Jesse Owens.

Hitler's earlier actions had certainly not been in keeping with Olympic protocol. As head of state he was the patron of the Games, but not part of the Olympic framework. Count Baillet-Latour pointed out that Hitler could receive medal winners only if he was prepared to greet every one; and since that was obviously impossible, he should receive no more. Whether the IOC president's action was born out of the fact that Hitler had walked out without meeting Johnson and Albritton, or simply because he thought that the Führer was taking too much upon himself, or that it was just against Olympic etiquette, is again open to debate.

It is difficult to imagine that, even had Baillet-Latour not laid down the law, Owens would have been invited to meet Adolf Hitler. In the VIP box with Hitler was Baldur von Schirach, leader of the Hitler Youth. Thirty years later, von Schirach claimed that the Führer had ranted on that the Americans should have been ashamed of themselves for 'letting negroes win medals for them'. According to von Schirach, both he and von Tschammer und Osten had suggested that a photograph of the Führer with Owens would be a good public relations move. Hitler had snarled back: 'Do you really think that I will allow myself to be photographed shaking hands with a negro?' Von Schirach's account, published in 1967, has him telling Hitler that it was up to the Americans who they chose to compete, and in any case, Owens was a 'friendly and educated man, a college student'. Given all that had passed before in Nazi Germany, and the furore surrounding a possible American boycott of the Games, if this account is true, then the Hitler Youth leader was either incredibly naïve or remarkably stupid. Or perhaps by the mid-1960s he was just very keen to rehabilitate his image, having spent twenty years in prison after being convicted at the Nuremburg war crimes trials.

American newspapers were quick to react to the fact that the country's black athletes had not been accorded the same recognition as had white European athletes. The *New York Times* headline ran: 'Hitler ignores Negro medalists'. The *New York Evening Journal* proclaimed:

> Chancellor Hitler, who has yet to pay homage to any of the negroes whose spectacular performance has done more than any other single factor to make these the greatest Olympics in history, left the stadium immediately after the conclusion of [Owens's] race.

And the African-American newspaper in Cleveland, the *Call and Post*, focused only on Owens and ran a huge headline: 'Hitler Snubs Jesse'. Other black newspapers, such as the *Baltimore Afro-American* and the *Chicago Defender*, took a similar line. Thereafter, every medal won by Owens – and 'ignored' by Hitler – simply added fuel to the fire. Owens himself was always happy to acknowledge that he had received a warm reception from German spectators at least, who even went so far as to chant his name: 'Yess-say ... Oh-vens ... Yess-say ... Oh-vens'. And for a long time he was also ready to point out that he, personally, had never been snubbed by Hitler. Eventually, however, constant denial became too much trouble and Owens just went along with the story. Later, he would say that he was so upset by Hitler's theories of a 'master race' that he fouled on the long-jump take-off board.

Whatever the truth behind Hitler's 'snub' to black athletes, the issue at least served to underline the nature of the Olympic hosts. In the wrestling hall, Germany's Werner Seelenbinder, a staunch Communist, had finished fourth in the Greco-Roman light-heavyweight division and was thus denied the opportunity to mount the winners' podium and defy Hitler by not giving the Nazi salute. After war was declared in September 1939, Seelenbinder joined the resistance movement and was arrested in 1942. After two years of torture, he was beheaded in Brandenburg prison.

Chapter Twelve

Gold Standard

Berlin was in a carnival mood. Everywhere in the Olympic city, bars and restaurants were crowded with Germans and foreign visitors. All public buildings, and most business premises, were festooned with flowers, Olympic symbols – and the swastika. While newcomers to the German capital were impressed, sometimes overwhelmed, by the splendour, especially along Unter den Linden, at the same time they could never escape the uniformed troops who always seemed to be marching here and there. And when it wasn't soldiers tramping through the streets, it was a parade of young boys and girls in uniform. Hotel lobbies never seemed short of their share of visiting officers, jackbooted and decorated with swastika badges and armbands, standing around smoking and gossiping.

Whenever Esther Myers and her fellow American students asked their new-found German friends what they felt about Hitler, they were generally asked not to mention the Führer. Similarly, if asked whether they were members of the National Socialist Party, those who were not usually answered in a whisper and then quickly changed the subject. There were plenty of people who were Nazi Party members, however, or at least supported its ideals. Whenever Hitler made his way up the Via Triumphalis towards the Olympic Stadium, there were always huge crowds lining the way. And there was always an equal number to salute the Führer when he left the stadium and made his way back to the Reich Chancellery, where armed SS guards in their black uniforms motioned people to cross to the other side of the street; no one was allowed to walk immediately in front of Hitler's official residence.

Whether his visits to the stadium took into account the likely successes of America's black athletes has never been established, but for one of them in particular, the third day of competition – Tuesday, 4 August – promised to be a particularly gruelling. Jesse Owens was entered into both the 200 m and the long jump, and both were scheduled to begin at 10.30 a.m. Owens, who had run 21.0 seconds in New York on 12 July that year – a world record time not ratified by the IAAF – was drawn in the third heat of the longer sprint and won easily, setting a new Olympic record of 21.1 seconds, a time he equalled in the third heat of the second round that afternoon. In between his 200 m heats, Owens made his way to the long-jump pit and a first competitive encounter with Lutz Long, a tall, blond-haired, blue-eyed 23-year-old from Leipzig, upon whose typically Aryan frame rested all German hopes for an event dominated by America since the first very modern Olympics.

As the world record holder, Owens was expected to maintain the American record of a gold medal in every Olympic long jump save 1920, when a Swede, William Petersson-Björneman, had briefly interrupted their reign. Owens jogged up the take-off board for a practice run without even attempting a leap. To his astonishment, a red flag was raised; a German official had ruled this perfunctory effort as an official – and illegal – jump. Ten minutes later, Owens tried again, this time fully focused. He hit the board and sailed well beyond the qualifying mark of 7.15 m (23 ft 5 ins). Again the same official raised his red flag, indicating to Owens that he had overstepped the line. Owens's coach, Larry Snyder, could barely conceal his fury; the athlete himself just looked puzzled. He had already fouled twice and had only one more opportunity to stay in the competition. Then Lutz Long came over. He reminded Owens that he was the world record holder; even if he jumped from well behind the board, surely he would still make the qualifying

With a new Olympic record long jump of 8.06m, Jesse Owens wins his second gold medal of the Games. (*Author's collection*)

distance which was a metre less than Owens had jumped in Ann Arbor a year earlier. Long even remeasured Owens's steps, then laid out his own sweatshirt alongside the take-off board as an added marker. Owens took off short of the board and still landed 60 cm past the qualifying distance, only this time there was no opportunity for a red flag. Then he made his way back to the track to ease into the 200 m semi-finals before returning to the long jump.

The world record stood at Owens's 8.13 m; the Olympic mark was 7.73 m, set by Ted Hamm in Amsterdam in 1928. Still wary after his experiences in the first round, but encouraged by the sportsmanship of his German rival, Owens took an early lead and after the first round of three jumps, both men had passed the old Olympic record, Owens going ahead with 7.87 m. Long had to settle for a new German and European record. With his first jump of the final round, Owens was again red-flagged; with his own second jump, Long hurtled towards the take-off board, leapt, and pedalled furiously to equal Owens's new record. Again the crowd erupted;

Lutz Long, whose massive effort in his final jump saw him foul, leaving Owens free to try for a new record. (*Author's collection*)

Owens congratulated Long, and then, when the noise had died down, began to focus on his own second jump. Just as in the sprints, Owens blotted out every outside distraction and directed everything into his task. Then he galloped towards the board, each stride longer than the last. It was a clean take-off – and a yet another Olympic record: 7.94.

Long now needed a superhuman effort with his final jump. The stadium fell hushed, Hitler stared intently through his binoculars, and Long summoned up every last reserve of energy, every last bit of concentration. Then he was off, the crowd now willing him on, screaming his name. Long landed on his stomach and before he could twist himself around he knew he had failed, the groans of the crowd told him that; another red flag had been raised. Jesse Owens had just won his second Olympic title in as many days. Owens still had one jump to come and, now freed from the fear of failure, he flew down the approach, hit the board cleanly, and hitch-kicked his way over all the previous marks to extend his Olympic record to 8.06 m (26 ft 5 in), just 7 cm short of his world best.

The first person to congratulate him was Long. 'You can melt down all the medals and cups I have,' Owens wrote later, 'and that wouldn't be a plating on the 24-carat friendship I felt for Lutz Long at that moment.'

By the time this day was done, others had joined Owens in gold medal glory. In the 800 m metres final, the long-legged 19-year-old African-American, John Woodruff, started as favourite but was last after 50 m, led at 200 m, then again fell to the rear at the halfway mark before his powerful sprint finish took him ahead of Mario Lanzi of Italy and Phil Edwards of Canada; Woodruff's 1 minute 52.9 seconds was the slowest winning Olympic time since 1920. On the winners' podium, Woodruff kept his hands clasped in front of him. Both Lanzi and Edwards gave what looked like a fascist salute, although as a black athlete, Edwards – born in British Guiana, later to become one of the world's leading experts on tropical diseases and here taking part in his third Games with bronze every time – was almost certainly giving the Olympic version; whichever, it painted an odd picture.

The best of friends: Owens and Long. (*Author's collection*)

John Woodruff (second from the right) gains ground on Canada's Phil Edwards to win the 800m final. (*Author's collection*)

Glenn Hardin, world and Olympic 400m record holder (left), pictured with John Loaring of Canada, who won the silver. (*Author's collection*)

In the 400 m hurdles, no one was surprised when the American Glenn Hardin world and Olympic record holder, won gold in 52.4 seconds. In addition to his running speed – he had covered the same distance flat in 49 seconds – Hardin's hurdling technique was superior to any other. John Loaring of Canada and Miguel White of the Philippine Islands followed him home. The last medals of the day were in the women's discus, where there was a double German triumph, Gisela Mauermayer and Paula Mollenhauer taking gold and bronze respectively, with Poland's Jadwiga Wajsówna winning the silver. Mauermayer, who was waiting for her world record of 48.31 m to be ratified, was again no surprise winner, her first throw of the final soaring 7 m beyond the old Olympic record.

Gisela Mauermayer (left) and Paula Mollenhauer, Germany's gold and bronze medallists in the women's shot put. (*Author's collection*)

The following afternoon, the recently knighted British Conservative MP, Henry 'Chips' Channon, arrived in Berlin. The American-born Channon had inherited enough money for him never to have to work again; he and his wife, a Guinness heiress, ran one of the most hospitable houses in London. Now, the Channons were in Berlin to be themselves entertained by the old aristocracy and the new regime. On the afternoon of their arrival, they went for a walk. In his diary, Channon wrote:

> Berlin was crowded with foreigners and the streets beflagged. Honor and I went for a walk down the Unter den Linden, an avenue of banners blowing in the breeze, and everywhere we heard the radio booming 'Achtung', and then giving the latest Olympic result.

When he eventually visited the Reich Sports Field he found the Games 'boring … and it was hot and dusty'.

On the cool Wednesday afternoon, however, Jesse Owens moved into the final of the 200 m, winning his heat in 21.3 seconds. In the other semi-final, his fellow African-American, Mack Robinson, equalled Owens's Olympic record set the previous day. It was clearly going to be an exciting final. Mack Robinson was the elder brother of Jackie Robinson, the player who, after the Second World War, broke the unstated but implacable colour bar in American Major League Baseball. Diagnosis of a heart murmur had almost ended Mack's athletic career before it had properly begun, but he overcame this to earn a place in the American team for Berlin. The 200 m finalists lined up under a threatening sky at just before 6.00 p.m.: Martinus Osendarp of Holland in the inside lane, then fellow Dutchman, Wijnand van Beveren, then Owens and Robinson, with Paul Hänni of Switzerland and Lee Orr of Canada on the outside. The two Americans were fastest off their marks, neck and neck for the first 100 m, but then Owens drew away for gold, leaving Robinson to fight off a mighty challenge from Osendarp. At the tape, Owens was 4 m ahead, his time a new Olympic and world record: 20.7 seconds.

Before the Games, Mack Robinson had been a star of the 1936 Oregon track team, winning Pacific Coast titles in the low hurdles and long jump, as well as an AAU national title at 200 m. None of that, nor his Olympic silver medal, counted for anything after he returned home. Expecting a hero's welcome when he arrived back in Pasadena, he was instead given the sort of job the city would have handed out to any other black: they gave him a broom and a cart and put him on the night shift as a street sweeper. Instead of having a parade in his honour, he would clear up the streets after others' parades. Sometimes he would wear his leather USA Olympic jacket to work. When criticized for such a provocative act, he would declare: 'When it was a cold day, it was the warmest thing I owned.' In 1984, he told George Beres, sports information director at the University of Oregon, that while American team members were not segregated in Berlin: 'We were segregated when we returned home, whites in one hotel, blacks in another. They let us know we were back in America, and that your place is "here," and the whites' place is "there." '

And while Jesse Owens did receive ticker tape welcomes, in New York and Cleveland, he, too, might have felt snubbed, not by the Chancellor of Germany, but by his own American president. Franklin Delano Roosevelt neither invited one of the greatest of all Olympians to the White House, nor even sent him a congratulatory letter or telegram. The AAU also paid him little respect. Even as Hitler was sweeping into the Olympic Stadium for the close of the Games, Owens was being suspended for refusing to travel to Scandinavia as part of a barnstorming, moneymaking – for the

AAU, not the athletes – tour of Europe. Later in the year, they bypassed the four-times Olympic champion for the Sullivan Award which 'honours America's top amateur athlete'; Glenn Morris, the Olympic decathlon champion, was chosen instead. That was no surprise to Owens; in 1935, the year he was stacking up new world records, the award had gone to champion golfer W Lawson Little Jr.

Late in the evening of Owens's triumphant day, the final of the men's pole vault reached a thrilling climax under floodlights as more than 25,000 spectators stayed on to brave the chilly night air. The American Earle Meadows and the Japanese pair, Shuhei Nishida and Sueo Oe, battled it out to exhaustion before Meadows won the gold with a new Olympic record of 4.35 m (14 ft 3 in). Nishida and Sueo, both on 4.25 m, refused to vault off for second and third place and their position was decided by drawing lots, with Nishida taking the silver. When they returned to Japan, they had a jeweller cut the medals in half and fuse them back together so that each man had half silver and half bronze. Earlier, there had been yet another American gold medal – and another Olympic record – when Kenneth

Shuhei Nishida of Japan in action during the early stages of the pole vault. By the time America's Earle Meadows had won gold with a new Olympic record, darkness had fallen on the Olympic Stadium.
(Author's collection)

Carpenter achieved 50.48 m in the discus after the favourites, Harald Andersson of Sweden, who was injured, and Willy Schröder of Germany, failed to rise to the occasion. Instead, Carpenter had to overcome the challenges of his teammate, Gordon Dunn, and the Giorgio Oberwerger of Italy. The left-handed Reidar Sørlie of Norway, who cut a comical figure in what looked like a pair of baggy gardening trousers, was in fourth place.

The fourth day of competition had also been a good one for the British contingent, whose morale was boosted by a courageous performance from Harold Whitlock, a London motor-car engineer. In October 1935, at the White City, Whitlock had broken the world record for the 30-mile walk; he then continued for another 3½ hours to break the 8-hour record, covering 51 miles, 1,042 yards around

Earle Meadows signs his autograph for a young admirer. Mississippi-born Meadows was a star of the University of Southern California track and field team. (*Author's collection*)

Kenneth Carpenter, another University of Southern California athlete, won gold in the discus. (*Author's collection*)

the White City track. It was the climax to a punishing schedule that year, for the Belgrave Harrier had entered almost every big race in England. He arrived in Berlin as one of the favourites for the 50 km walk, the British title of which he would hold from 1934 to the outbreak of war. Whitlock's main rivals would be Arthur Schwab of Switzerland, who held several records, Adalberts Bubenko of Latvia, and Stork of Czechoslovakia.

The course was about 40 km of tarmacked roads and about 10 km of asphalt or stone pavement. Almost 42 km were in the shade, with the steepest gradient 30 m per 1 km at the Grunewald Tower. A brief shower two hours before the start made the course slightly damp, and under overcast skies and in temperatures around 64°F, the walkers set off at 1.30 p.m. After letting Stork and Janis Dalinsch (Latvia) make the early pace, Whitlock moved into the lead at the 33 km mark, but 5 km later he began to vomit, almost certainly due to the sickly tea made with condensed milk that he had been given instead of his usual glucose mixture at 25 km; Whitlock had taken only a couple of gulps before throwing away the disgusting concoction, but it was now making him feel ill. Throwing up the tea soon had a beneficial effect, however, and at 45 km he was steadily increasing his lead, crossing the finishing line in 4 hours, 30 minutes and 41.4 seconds, a new Olympic record. One week later, Whitlock was back home, greeted by the townsfolk of Deptford who gave their gold medallist a hero's welcome.

Thursday 6 August saw the last of the cool, cloudy, often showery weather that had dogged these Olympics, although it was not until about 6.30 p.m. that the wind finally fell and the skies cleared to leave just high, thin 'mare's tails' cloud. During the early afternoon, the crowd had become agitated as a large, rotund man in a white uniform appeared in the VIP box; Hermann Göring had arrived. The crowd stood up and saluted. An hour or so later, they were on their feet again, this time roaring their appreciation: Hitler himself had arrived.

London motor mechanic Harold Whitlock on his way to gold in the 50km walk, despite becoming ill during the race. (*Author's collection*)

At 4.15 p.m. came one of the most eagerly awaited events of the Games: the final of the men's 1500 m, the so-called 'metric mile'. Usually, a race will have its out-and-out favourite; occasionally, almost the entire field will be of such a high standard that the prospect of seeing them compete is positively mouth-watering. The 1936 Olympic 1500 m was such a race. A fast time was guaranteed by the presence of three men. Luigi Beccali of Italy was the defending Olympic champion and record holder. Glenn Cunningham, the 'Iron Man of Kanas', held the world record for the mile, which was a remarkable achievement considering that in 1917, when he was 8 years old, Cunningham had suffered a badly burned leg in a schoolhouse fire in which his brother had died. The last member of this great triumvirate was Jack Lovelock, a slight, crinkly-haired New Zealander with a shy smile. The event was an

The start of the men's 1500m, the so-called 'metric mile'. (*Author's collection*)

ever-changing scene: Lovelock had set a new world record in the 1933 Mile of the Century at Princeton's Palmer Stadium in New Jersey; then Cunningham had broken that record in the 1934 race; and in 1935, Lovelock had beaten Cunningham in the same Princeton event, on what was then one of the fastest tracks in the world.

There would have been the prospect of an even more fascinating Olympic 1500 m, but for the fact that Britain's great hope, Sydney Wooderson, struggling to shake off an ankle injury, had been eliminated in one of the heats. Wooderson's presence would have added a delicious new dimension. Still a few days short of his 22nd birthday, his appearance – he stood 5 ft 6 in tall, weighed less than 9 stone and wore spectacles – belied his talent. Three times Wooderson had beaten Lovelock, most sensationally in the 1935 AAA's championships, a feat which he repeated the following year. Photographs of both races show Lovelock smiling as Wooderson breasts the tape, almost as if the New Zealander is trying to work out how this small, pale man in spectacles has beaten the Kiwi's famed sprint finish. A former Rhodes Scholar and, at the time of the Olympics, a medical student, Lovelock had run tests on himself to ascertain how he could sustain a fast finish in different conditions.

From left to right, the runners in the 1500 m are: Eric Ny, Jack Lovelock, Glenn Cunningham, Luigi Beccali, Phil Edwards, Jerry Cornes, Miklos Szabo, Gene Venzke. Lovelock won in a new world record time. Great Britain's Jerry Cornes had been posted to Nigeria in 1932 – going via the Los Angeles Olympics where he won a silver medal – and needed special leave to compete in 1936. (*Author's collection*)

It was a strategy which would prove devastatingly effective in Berlin. For the first three-quarters of the race there was a great deal of jockeying for position as runners tried to mentally press the opposition while still reserving enough for their own final burst. Cunningham took over the lead at 400 m, followed by Lovelock. The New Zealander dropped back to fourth, and just before the bell which signalled the start of the last lap, Eric Ny of Sweden went in front. With 300 m to run, Lovelock had come back up to second place behind the Swede. Cunningham followed him, then hesitated, thinking that Lovelock's surge had been a bluff. That was the precise moment for which Lovelock had planned. He now accelerated away. Cunningham was shocked; Lovelock had never delivered his kick this early, and now he had to hold it. Ny faded and although Cunningham and Beccali gave chase it was to no avail. Lovelock blistered down the track for New Zealand's first Olympic gold in athletics. His time of 3 minutes 47.8 seconds – equivalent to a mile in 4 minutes 4.8 seconds – was a new world record. Cunningham, 5 m behind, had also passed the old record;

even Beccali, in the bronze medal position, was only four-tenths of a second outside the old mark.

Harold Abrahams, a 1924 gold-medal-winning Olympian, was commentating for the BBC and got very excited, so much so that it was not until the final few metres that he was absolutely certain about who was winning: 'A hundred yards to go! Come on, Jack! My God, he's done it. Jack, come on! ... Lovelock wins. Five yards, six yards, he wins. He's won. Hooray!' In the *Manchester Guardian*, E A Montague had time to give a more considered response: 'It was a race magnificent beyond all description ... There never was such a run, nor such a runner.'

After the clutch of gold medals and Olympic records achieved by African-American athletes, victory by a white runner, even if he wasn't German, would certainly have pleased the Nazi hosts. *Der Angriff* (The Attack), the newspaper founded by Goebbels shortly after he took over as the party's district leader in Berlin, complained: 'If the American team had not brought along black auxiliaries ... one would have regarded the Yankees as the biggest disappointment of the Games.' The paper argued that, but for the blacks, Long would have won the long jump, Osendarp the 100 m, Lanzi the 800 m.

Forrest Towns (second from the right) is focused on the finishing line in the 110m hurdles. (*Author's collection*)

They could have no argument about the 110 m hurdles, the final of which was run an hour and a half after Lovelock's great victory. In the earlier stages, Forrest 'Spec' Towns had set a new Olympic record of 14.1 seconds, which equalled his world record in Chicago in June that year. And he was a white man, the first person from the American state of Georgia to take part in the Olympics. His record-breaking time in the semi-finals made him the favourite for a gold medal, but until the fourth hurdle had been crossed, he was led by his countryman, Fred Pollard. Then Towns took over, winning the gold just one-tenth of a second outside his own world record; as he crossed the line he clasped his hands together above his head, pumping them in a victory salute. Pollard, however, stumbled at the last hurdle, giving silver to the British team captain, the RAF officer Don Finlay. At a post-Olympic race in Oslo, Towns was to set yet another new world record with an unbelievable 13.7 seconds. His time might have been due to the fact that, like Owens, he was annoyed at being made to take part in the AAU tour when all he really wanted to do was go home to join the University of Georgia football team. Former Georgia athletic director H J Stegeman, who attended the 1936 Olympics and wrote a series of columns for the *Athens Banner-Herald*, said of Towns:

> He is a great competitor and can be relied upon to do his best when necessary. He is refreshingly modest in spite of his fame. His conduct is exemplary, and he shares his enthusiasm with everyone, including his competitors.

Gerhard Stöck, bronze medallist in the shot, earned another gold for Germany, with a winning throw of 71.84 m in the javelin as Göring and Goebbels applauded furiously. In the triple jump, Japan's bespectacled youngster Naoto Tajima, who two days earlier had taken bronze in the long jump, won the gold with a world record hop, step and jump of 16 m. Lutz Long, the long-jump silver

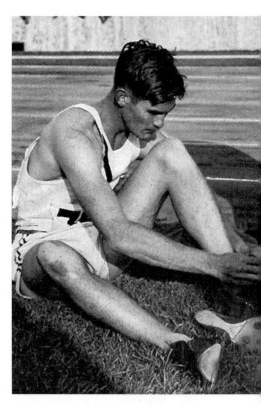

Forrest Towns set a new Olympic record and equalled his own world record.
(*Author's collection*)

Gerhard Stöck won gold for Germany in the javelin; Goebbels applauded furiously. (*Author's collection*)

medallist, finished tenth in the triple jump. In the women's 80 m hurdles, there was a long delay before Trebisonda Valla of Italy was declared the winner. Valla, Anni Steuer of Germany and Canada's Elizabeth Taylor had reached the tape practically simultaneously, all timed at 11.7 seconds. The judges spent half an hour peering at the photograph before announcing their verdict. In an earlier round, Valla had run a wind-assisted 11.6 seconds which equalled the Olympic record but was declared invalid as a new world mark.

Friday, 7 August dawned brighter and warmer than at any time since the opening ceremony. Towards midday, the clouds began to roll back and there were even a few spots of rain but, with temperatures now edging towards 70°F, conditions were much more pleasant. For three Britons in particular, it was a hugely important day: Godfrey Brown, Godfrey Rampling and Bill Roberts were all running in the semi-finals of the 400 m. Brown, the Indian-born Cambridge University student, was favourite for a medal, but Rampling and Roberts had also run under 48 seconds and all three were the best Europeans at the distance. Rampling was an army officer; at the 1932 Games he had anchored the 4 × 400 m relay team which won the silver medal behind the United States. In 1945 he would become the proud father of a baby girl called Charlotte, today one of Britain's best-known actresses. Roberts, from Salford in Lancashire, had finished second behind Rampling in the 440 yds at the 1934 Empire Games.

In the first heat, the African-American Archie Williams – who before 1936 had never run a quarter-mile faster than 49 seconds – won in 47.2 seconds, with Roberts in second place. In the second race, another African-American, James Lu Valle, won in 47.1 with Brown coming second. Rampling, though, finished fourth and was eliminated. The final was a thriller. Brown's bad luck in the draw continued when he was in the outside lane; Roberts was drawn in lane 3. For the first 100 m, Brown led, but then Williams and Lu Valle broke away. Entering the home stretch, Williams was out in front, but Brown fought back and all but caught the American at the tape. Williams looked to be faltering as he crossed the line in 46.5 seconds, but the race was 400 m, not 10 m metres more; had it been, then Britain might have had another gold medal. As it was, they had to settle for

Archie Williams, a graduate of the University of California, was a virtual unknown when he set a new world record in the 400m at the 1936 NCAA championships. A few weeks later he would collect an Olympic gold medal. *(Author's collection)*

silver; Lu Valle had just held off Roberts for the bronze, although they were both timed at 46.8 seconds. The following day, Brown's sister, Audrey, made it a double silver for the family as a member of the British women's 4 × 100 m relay team.

While the decathletes were midway through deciding five of their events – 100 m, 400 m, long jump, high jump and shot put – the final of the 5000 m got under way at just after 3.15 p.m. Britain had two representatives, Peter Ward and Frank Close, neither of whom were fancied against the Finns, Gunnar Höckert and Lauri Lehtinen, or Sweden's John Jonsson. The Americans had only one runner, Louis Zamperini, a former juvenile delinquent from California whose life had been rescued, as over the years has that

In the 400m final, Williams of the USA comes home ahead of Britain's Godfrey Brown and James Lu Vale (USA). (*Author's collection*)

Finland's Volmari Iso-Hollo leads the field in the 3000m steeplechase on his way to gold and a new world record. (*Author's collection*)

of many young men, by an athletic ability. Nineteen-years-old, Zamperini had stepped aboard the SS *Manhattan* for the journey across the Atlantic, an awe-struck young man. For a start, he had never seen so much food and had put on 12 lbs by the time he arrived in Berlin. In the 5000 m final, Zamperini did not win any medals for America – with two laps remaining the 10,000 m champion, Ilmari Salminen, tripped on his fellow Finn, Lauri Lehtinen, and let in yet another Finn, Gunnar Höckert, for the gold – but he did catch Hitler's eye.

Thanks to an impressive last lap of around 56 seconds Zamperini came in eighth and the Führer asked to meet 'the American with the fast finish'. Asked later what he thought of him, Zamperini replied: 'Even if Hitler had given me his wristwatch it wouldn't have meant much. He was just another dictator. At the time I didn't understand politics, and was more concerned about other things than how the world worked – or didn't.' Zamperini caught the eye again when he tried to steal a swastika flag as a souvenir. There were angry shouts and suddenly Zamperini and a friend found themselves surrounded by armed soldiers. Why had he done such a thing, asked an officer. 'Because I wanted a souvenir of the wonderful time I've had in Germany,' replied the American. The German gave him back the flag. Even then, Louis Zamperini's remarkable life experiences were far from over. Shot down over the Pacific while serving as a USAAF bomb-aimer, he survived for 47 days adrift on a raft, and two and a half years as a prisoner of the Japanese. Ironically, he had been looking forward to the 1940 Olympics in Tokyo.

One week after the remarkable opening ceremony of the Games, Berlin awoke to another Saturday of military bands and the tramp of marching soldiers. In the Olympic Stadium the track and field athletics were drawing to their close, with the final of the 3000 m steeplechase and the last events in the decathlon scheduled for this penultimate day. In the steeplechase, a new type of hurdle was being used. The hurdles used in 1928 and 1932 had been too light; there was always a danger that they would fall over when the runners knocked against them. In Berlin, a heavier hurdle with cross-pieces 12 cm wide was being tried. It proved popular with the runners, who could jump on to the hurdle, then down from it, if they no longer had enough strength to clear it altogether. Again Finland demonstrated her ability in long-distance running. The elimination heats had revealed that the 1932 gold medallist, Volmar Iso-Hollo, had lost none of his form. In the final he went straight into the lead, followed by his fellow Finns, Matti Matilainen and

Kaarlo Tuominen. In the penultimate lap Iso-Hollo left the field behind while his compatriots seemed to have secured silver and bronze. Then Alfred Dompert of Germany began to overtake them. Mattilainen hung on for silver, but Tuominen was forced to let the German pass him. Iso-Hollo's time of 9 minutes 3.8 seconds was a new world record; in fact the first three all passed the old mark set by America's Harold Manning, who finished fifth behind Tuominen in this race.

The steeplechase had begun at 4.00 p.m., as the decathlon was reaching its climax. The final event, the 1500 m, was due to begin at 5.30 p.m. and was run in three heats. Just before the first heat it was announced that Glenn Morris, a car salesman from Colorado, needed to run the race in no more than 4 minutes 32 seconds to set a new world record. The American was disappointed; it was 16 seconds faster than he had had ever run in his life. In the early stages of the decathlon, another American, Bob Clark, had taken the lead, but Morris had advanced with each event until at the end of the eighth, the pole vault, he was leading with 6,633 points,

America's champion decathletes, from left to right: Bob Clark (silver), Glenn Morris (gold) and Jack Parker (bronze). (*Author's collection*)

followed by Clark with 6,480 and Jack Parker (also the USA) with 6,194. The ninth competition, javelin-throwing, enabled Morris to increase his total to 7,305 points and he would surely now be crowned champion; but the world record looked well outside his grasp. Nevertheless, he made a gigantic effort to win in 4 minutes 33.2 seconds. Then it was announced that a computing error had been made. Not only had he won the gold medal – in only his third decathlon – he had also achieved a new world record with 7,900 points. Clark took the silver, Parker the bronze. Morris later had a brief but passionate affair with Hitler's favourite film-maker, Leni Riefenstahl. He also had a Hollywood career, if that is what it can be called, appearing in two excruciatingly bad movies, *Tarzan's Revenge* (in which he inevitably played Tarzan) and *Hold That Co-Ed*, as well as playing himself in *Decathlon Champion: The Story of Glenn Morris*.

All this was in the future, however. First Morris and his fellow decathletes, their own job done, could rest and enjoy the final day of track and field competition. Sunday 9 August promised the climax of the marathon, the women's high jump and 4 × 100 m relay, and the men's 4 × 400 m and 4 × 100 m relays, which meant a return to the arena for Jesse Owens, but in the most controversial of circumstances. For several weeks it had been assumed that the American team would comprise Sam Stoller, Marty Glickman, Frank Wykoff and Foy Draper. At the US trials at Randall's Island, New York, Stoller had finished sixth in the 100 m, just behind Glickman. The first three finishers made the team in that event, the next four qualifying as members of the relay team. Stoller would run the lead-off leg, Glickman the back stretch, Draper the turn, and Wykoff the anchor leg. For ten days after their arrival in Berlin – the American team had landed at Hamburg on 24 July and travelled on to the German capital by train – the quartet practised hard. On the evening of 5 August, after Jesse Owens had won the 200 m, coach Lawson Robertson was asked if Owens would be added to the relay team. Robertson's reply was unambiguous: Owens had collected enough

The giant scoreboard shows America's triple triumph in the decathlon. (*Author's collection*)

After his fourth gold medal of the 1936 Games, the Olympic triumphs of Jesse Owens are immortalized in stone at the stadium. (*Author's collection*)

gold medals and small oak trees; the other boys deserved their chance.

On the morning of the heats, however, Glickman and Stoller – both Jewish – were told that they were being replaced by Owens and Metcalfe. There was a rumour, said Robertson, that Germany had kept two 'super sprinters' in reserve; he had to field his strongest team. Owens protested but was ordered to do as he was told. Glickman also protested, pointing out that, since he and Stoller were the only Jews on the American team, there was bound to be an uproar back home. In his diary, the 21-year-old Stoller recorded that it was 'the most humiliating episode in my life'. The change in personnel made little sense in sporting terms. Owens and Metcalfe were both faster runners, true, but both Stoller and Glickman had beaten Draper, the white non-Jew, and at least one of them should have run in his place. There were the inevitable claims that it was a decision based purely on anti-Semitism. 'The only way we could have lost that race is if we had dropped the baton,' said Glickman. Avery Brundage was accused of wanting to spare Hitler the embarrassment of two Jews on the winners' podium, a charge which the American Olympic Committee president described as 'absurd'. The official IOC report contented itself with: 'In the case of this event, America abandoned her customary practice of entering only fresh runners in the relays and made use of her outstanding sprinters.'

In the event, the American team won the 4×100 m relay – and Owens his fourth gold medal of the Games – in 39.8 seconds, a world record that would last for twenty years. Even in the heats the four Americans had equalled the old world record, and in the final Owens established a lead which his countrymen increased at will. For Wykoff it was a third straight gold relay medal, setting a world record every time. Italy gained silver in 41.1 seconds. Germany moved up to third when Holland was disqualified because their final runner, Osendarp, had dropped the baton 15 m from the finish. When the US track team competed at post-Games meets in Paris and London. Glickman was reinstated to the relay team, but Stoller, bitterly disappointed by the Berlin snub, returned home immediately. Fifty years later, Glickman revisited the Berlin stadium where he had been denied his chance of Olympic glory. He told the *New York Times*:

> I stopped and looked across to the far side where Hitler and his entourage had watched the Games ... Suddenly a wave of rage overwhelmed me ... I began to scream every dirty curse word, every obscenity I knew ... being there, visualizing and reliving those moments, caused the eruption which had been gnawing at me for so long and which I thought I had expunged years ago.

In 1998, William J. Hyde, president of the US Olympic Committee, presented Glickman and Stoller (posthumously; he had died in 1983) with a special plaque 'in lieu of the gold medals they didn't win'.

If the Americans had been seriously concerned about fielding the best possible teams, they did not show it only half an hour after the revamped 4×100 m line-up had won gold. In the 4×400 m relay, they stuck to their original foursome, ignoring medal winners Archie Williams and James Lu Valle. Given that the British approach was somewhat cavalier – Rampling recalled that they practised baton-changing, 'but soon got bored and packed it in' – it might not have mattered. But the Americans, Cagle, Young, O'Brien and Fitsch, were soundly defeated by Wolff, Rampling, Roberts and Brown who earned Britain a rare athletics gold. Freddie Wolff was

8 m behind at the first changeover, and with Canada's Phil Edwards running the second leg, it seemed all up for British hopes. But Rampling was more than equal to the challenge, forging first past Young and then Edwards to hand Roberts a 2 m-lead. The Salford AC man, who had learned his craft in hell-for-leather races on makeshift rough grass tracks around Manchester, extended that lead, and so did Brown who was running the anchor leg. The winning margin was 11 m, the time 3 minutes 9 seconds, less than a second outside the world record. Germany and Canada contested the bronze medal, Harry Voigt, the third German runner, deciding the issue by establishing a decisive lead.

In between the men's relay races, the women's 4 × 100 m final had taken place, with another success for Britain. The Germans entered the final as one of the favourites after setting a new world record in the heats. They got off well, Emmy Albus giving them a clear advantage before handing over cleanly to Käthe Krauss. Marie Dollinger and Krauss achieved another perfect exchange and Dollinger opened up a lead of several metres before the baton

The second change in the 4 x 400m relay. Great Britain's Bill Roberts receives the baton from Godfrey Rampling while the USA, Canada and Germany compete for second place. (*Author's collection*)

crossed to Ilse Dörffeldt for the last leg. The Americans had reserved their new sprinting sensation, Helen Stephens, for the final charge as 90,000 spectators, including Adolf Hitler, leapt to their feet. Then disaster struck: Dörffeldt had not taken a proper grip on the baton. It fell from her hand and hit the red clay. The German girl pulled up, her head in her hands, and Stephens was past her and out of sight for another American gold. Their time of 46.9 seconds was four-tenths of a second slower than Germany's world record in the heats. Hitler slumped back in his seat, then began to talk animatedly to those around him; he looked puzzled, shocked. Dörffeldt was devastated – so much so that the Führer was moved to invite her and her teammates into his box for official commiserations. Besides giving America the gold medal, however, Dörffeldt's blunder had let in Britain for silver. Eileen Hiscock, Violet Olney, Audrey Brown and Barbara Burke duly took their places on the podium, with Canada collecting a very unexpected bronze.

Dörffeldt's error cost the Germans dear, but they officially denied themselves a gold medal in the women's high jump after telling the Jewish Gretel Bergmann that her performances had been 'mediocre'. Bergmann had won the German trials with 1.64 m. Now Ibolya Csák was to win gold for Hungary with an inferior jump. Only Csák, Elfriede Kaun of Germany and a 16-year-old Briton, Dorothy Odam, succeeded in clearing the bar at 1.60 m. 'We want Dot to win!' chanted the British contingent, but all the women failed at 1.62 m so a jump-off was necessary. On her next attempt, Csák jumped 1.62 m while the others failed. The bar was then lowered to 1.60 m but the German failed to clear this, so the places were awarded to Csák, Odam (silver) and Kaun (bronze). In view of the fact that the Hungarian athlete had cleared 1.62 m only in the jump-off, this height was not recognized and she was awarded her gold for having jumped 1.60 m and, in addition, winning the jump-off. Under later tie-break rules Odam would have had the gold. Following their rejection

America's Helen Stephens is congratulated by high jumper Alice Arden after taking the USA to gold in the women's 4 × 100 m relay. (*Author's collection*)

Ibolya Csák (left), Hungary's gold medal women's high jumper, with Germany's Elfriede Kaun and the 16-year-old Briton, Dorothy Odam. (*Author's collection*)

Runners leave the stadium at the start of the marathon. (*Author's collection*)

of Bergmann, the Germans were so desperate for a medal in the women's high jump that they entered one Dora Ratjen. This athlete finished in fourth place, but in 1938 was barred from further competition after being examined and discovered to possess 'ambiguous genitalia'. In 1957, by now living as Hermann Ratjen, he admitted that the Nazis had forced him to enter as a woman.

While all this was taking place, the marathon race had been progressing. For this (42.195 km / 26 miles 385 yds long), the 100 km cycle race and the 50 km walk, the German Signal Corps had constructed an extensive telephone system to keep both judges and the general public informed. Signal Division 43 from Potsdam, partly by using public telephone lines, had installed eleven telephone stations along the marathon course. As the runners' route followed the same course on the outward and return journeys, it was thus possible to give twenty-two sectional reports.

Korea's Sohn Kee-chung, running as Kitei Son in the colours of Japan, breasts the tape at the end of the marathon. (*Author's collection*)

The defending champion, Juan Carlos Zabala of Argentina, had been in Berlin for months, training along the exact course and all the time probably thinking about Sohn Kee-chung of Korea, who in November 1935 had set a world record of 2 hours 26 minutes 42 seconds. In fact there was no entry for Sohn Kee-chung in the Berlin Games, but there was one for Kitei Son of Japan. They were one and the same man. Japan had occupied Korea and the only way for Sohn to take part in the Olympics was to run under the Rising Sun flag and under a Japanese version of his name. Zabala carried out his usual stock-in-trade – taking the lead straight away – and at the 4 km mark he was 30 seconds in front. At 15 km he had extended his lead to 1 minute 40 seconds, and after slipping a little he was still 90 seconds in front after 25 km. From the start, Sohn had been running with Ernie Harper, a 34-year-old coal miner from Sheffield, who ran for the Hallamshire Harriers club.

After 28 km, first Sohn, then Harper, passed the Argentinian who had run himself into the ground after such an aggressive start. Zabala fell, got up, and then 4 km later dropped out of the race. Sohn won by over two minutes, with Harper holding off another Japanese Korean import, Nam Seung-yong, to take the silver medal, despite a badly blistered foot which left him with a running shoe full of blood. Afterwards, Sohn said that that he would not have won but for Harper sportingly telling him not to chase after Zabala because he was setting too fast a pace. At the medal ceremony, Sohn was forced to watch the Japanese flag run up the winner's mast, and to listen to the Japanese national anthem. Both he and Nam lowered their heads in silent protest and Sohn refused to sign his Japanese name. He used the publicity as an opportunity to tell Western journalists of his country's plight; few, if any, were interested. Back home in Korea, however, he was given a hero's welcome, one newspaper publishing a photograph of him but only after the Japanese flag on his sweatshirt had been painted over. The Japanese responded by suspending the paper – *Dong-a-Ilbo* – for nine months and imprisoning several people connected with it. In 1948, Sohn Kee-chung carried his nation's flag at the London Olympics; forty years later he carried the torch into Seoul's Olympic Stadium before the start of the 1988 Summer Games.

Meanwhile, as the track and field events ended in Berlin, the Japanese were looking forward to 1940, when it would be their turn in Tokyo.

Oberstleutnant Gotthard Handrick finishes 14th in the 4000 m cross-country run, the last discipline of the modern pentathlon. However, Handrick's early lead in the other disciplines was enough to secure the gold medal. Flying a Messerschmitt Bf 109 with the Condor Legion in the Spanish Civil War, Handrick was credited with shooting down five aircraft. (*Author's collection*)

Chapter Thirteen

LAST HURRAHS

If everyone's focus had appeared to be on the Olympic Stadium and the glamour of the athletics, there was plenty of action taking place all around the Grunewald complex and further afield. Boxing, hockey, gymnastics, fencing, swimming, equestrian sports, yachting, rowing and much more – they were all as important to their competitors and supporters as any of the explosive events of track and field. Outside the stadium itself, the best supported events, so far as paying spectators were concerned, were polo on the May Field, hockey in its own stadium immediately adjoining the Olympic Stadium, boxing in the Deutschland Hall on Königsweg, gymnastics in the Dietrich Eckhart open-air theatre and swimming.

Work on the swimming stadium, which was built of natural limestone, had continued right up until the eve of competition. Originally it had been planned to increase the stadium's capacity by constructing additional rows of seats at the top and bottom of the permanent stands, but it also proved necessary to erect another complete stand at the north end. This meant that a splendid view of the green expanse of parkland was lost, but the wooden stand harmonized well with the rest of the stadium and, in the words of the IOC official report, 'the loss of view was amply compensated'. However, it was decided to erect stands at the southern end in order to give the stadium a still more enclosed appearance, and these were not completed until 7 August. The following day the swimming events began.

The decision to increase the stadium's capacity was amply justified. Throughout their eight days, the swimming events averaged a paying attendance of more than 14,500 each day. As expected the men's events were dominated by the Japanese – who won three of the six gold medals – and the Americans. Only the 22-year-old Hungarian medical student Ferenc Csik flew the flag for Europe, winning the 100 m freestyle in 57.6 seconds, the fastest time of his life. As the Americans – who included world record holder Peter Fick of the New York Athletic Club – and Japanese raced against other, Csik sneaked up from an outside lane to win the gold. Csik was killed in an air raid while serving as an army doctor in the Second World War. He was buried in the Csik

The swimming stadium at the Reich Sports Field. The decision to increase its capacity was soon justified by attendances of more than 14,500 each day. (*Author's collection*)

Ferenc Csik won the 100 m freestyle gold medal at the Berlin Games. Nine years later he was killed during an air raid. (*Author's collection*)

Ferenc Esplanade, a memorial sports ground near the floating swimming pool where he had learned to swim in his home town of Kesztheley.

In the women's events, Europe – or rather Holland – did do exceptionally well. The Dutch girl Rie Mastenbroek won gold medals (and set new Olympic records) in the 100 m and 400 m freestyle, silver in the 100 m backstroke and another gold in the 4 × 100 m relay. Her Dutch colleague, Nida Senff, won gold in the 100 m backstroke, so it was a wonderful Games for Holland in the swimming. Their strong women's relay team of Mastenbroek, Jopi Selbach, Tina Wagner and Willy den Ouden had trained – in a Rotterdam canal for distance and the pool for sprint work – under Mastenbroek's coach, the formidable Ma Braun. Mastenbroek's career was as short as it was sensational: in 1933 she was taking part in the Rotterdam regional championships; in 1935 she was a European champion; in 1936, still aged only 17, she was proclaimed the greatest women swimmer in the world. A year later, Mastenbroek, who broke nine world records – six for backstroke and three for freestyle – became a swimming instructor, a move that forced her to forfeit her amateur status, thereby becoming ineligible for further competition.

Senff, meanwhile, had been robbed of her chance to challenge the American Eleanor Holm, a world record holder in several events. At the time, Holm was married to the singer and band leader, Art Jarrett, and both led an active social life. On the SS *Manhattan*, which took the American team on the nine-day journey across the Atlantic, Holm did not take kindly to the third-class accommodation and strict regime imposed by the American Olympic Committee. On Friday, 17 July, she attended a party given by the ship's owners. She stayed up until dawn and had to be helped to her cabin. The American OC issued an official reprimand, but Holm thought she was untouchable. She continued to drink in public and when the ship docked at Cherbourg, she ignored orders to remain aboard and instead went out on the town. Late that evening, the team chaperone found Holm staggering along the quayside in the company of a young man. Taken back to her cabin, which she shared with teammates Mary Lou Petty and Olive McKean, Holm began to shout obscenities through a porthole. The team doctor was called and now found her fast asleep. Unable to rouse her, he conducted as good an examination as he could before returning a diagnosis of 'acute alcoholism'. The following day Holm was barred from the team. She appealed in vain and attended the Games as a spectator while taking full advantage of Berlin's night life. In 1972 she told *Sports Illustrated*: 'I enjoyed the parties, the uniforms, the flags ... Göring was fun.' When Senff beat Mastenbroek by three-tenths of a second in the 100 m backstroke, Eleanor Holm, who had not been defeated in a swimming pool for seven years, was watching from the best seats. In 1938, Holm starred opposite gold medal decathlete Glenn Morris in *Tarzan's Revenge*.

Events in the swimming stadium produced some other notable achievements. Thirteen-year-old Marjorie Gestring of America won gold in springboard diving; she remains the youngest female gold medallist in the history of the Summer Olympics. Inge Sørensen of Denmark earned a bronze medal in the 200 m breaststroke at the age of 12, making her the youngest medallist ever in an individual event. And the Hungarian water polo player, Olivér Halassy, won a gold medal – he had another gold from 1932 and had won silver in 1928 – despite the fact that one of his legs had been amputated below the knee following a tramcar accident.

If there were never any realistic hopes for a German success in the swimming, down in the Dietrich Eckhart amphitheatre almost everything the host nation touched turned to gold. The Germans' long tradition in competitive gymnastics ensured a crowd of nearly

The Dutch swimmer Rie Mastenbroek, is emotional after winning gold in the 100 m freestyle. Her coach, the redoubtable Ma Braun, permits herself a satisfied smile. (*Author's collection*)

Mastenbroek's colleague, Nida Senff, and her coach are delighted after Senff's gold in the 100 m backstroke. (*Author's collection*)

17,000 each day; the majority of spectators – seated on stone tiers in the manner of the audience at an ancient Greek play – were rewarded with six Olympic titles including the individual men's all-round and the team championship. Most of the action took place on a large stage covered by an awning of waterproof canvas, although by the time the gymnastics got under way on 10 August, the weather was perfect with almost clear skies, a gentle south-easterly breeze and temperatures a few degrees higher than normal for the month.

Until 1933, the German Gymnastic Association had been outside the International Gymnastic Federation (IGF). German gymnasts had competed in earlier Olympic Games, but as individuals. With the Games to be held in Berlin, that issue had to be addressed and at the 1934 world championships in Budapest, Germany was admitted to the IGF. For the first time, German men gymnasts competed as a group in an international contest. The 1936 Olympics offered German women gymnasts their first chance to test themselves at international level; they responded by winning gold in the only event for them: the combined exercises. The men

Gymnastics at the Dietrich Eckhart also attracted large crowds every day. (*Author's collection*)

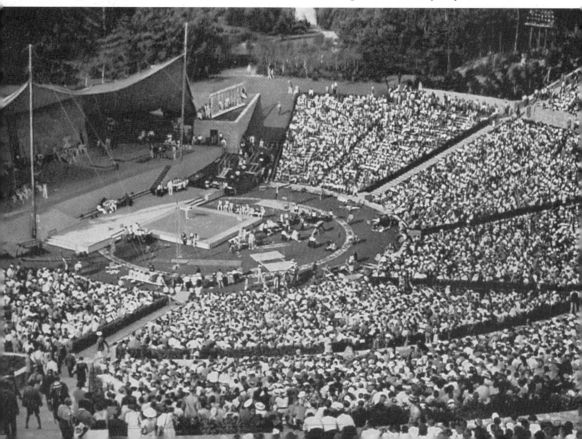

Alfred Schwarzmann, a Nuremburg baker, stands tall after winning the individual combined exercises. In front of him is bronze medallist and fellow German, Konrad Frey; behind him is the Swiss silver medallist, Eugene Mack. (*Author's collection*)

also dominated: Alfred Schwarzmann, a baker from Nuremburg, won the individual combined exercises and men's vault; Konrad Frey the parallel bars and pommel horse. The interruptions to a clean sweep came from a Czech gymnast, Alois Hudec, on the ring, Aleksanteri Saarvala of Finland on the parallel bars, and Sweden's Georges Miez in the floor exercises.

There had been no women's gymnastics at the 1932 Olympics, but in Amsterdam in 1928, Holland had won the women's combined exercises. Half their team were Jewish; four of them would perish at the hands of the Nazis. Along with her husband and 10-year-old daughter, Helena Nordheim was to die in a gas chamber at Sobibor concentration camp in July 1943. Anna Polak also died at Sobibor that month, together with her 6-year-old daughter. Judikje Simons (a reserve who did not compete) was killed at Sobibor in March 1943, together with her husband, 5-year-old daughter and 3-year-old son. Estella Agsterribe perished in an Auschwitz gas chamber in September 1943, together with her 2-year-old son and 6-year-

Konrad Frey took gold in the parallel bars and pommel horse. (*Author's collection*)

old daughter. Two members of the 1928 Dutch men's team, Mozes Jacobs and trainer Gerrit Kleerekoper, also perished at Sobibor in July 1943.

In the hockey stadium, meanwhile, Germany was coming unstuck against another race. However, the Nazis regarded Indians as being of Aryan descent so, despite their brown faces, their resounding victory over the host nation could be tolerated. The stadium normally accommodated 11,000 spectators – all but 2,000 of them standing – but for the Olympic Games temporary stands had been erected along its sides. These increased the capacity to 18,000 with standing room for 11,500 and 6,500 seats. Attendances averaged around 12,000, but for the final – Germany versus India – the stadium was tested to the full.

During their fifteen-day voyage to Germany, the Indians had lost hundreds of hockey balls while practising on the deck of the liner *Aitheneaver*. One day after their arrival in Berlin, India played a warm-up game against a German side and lost 4–1. A cable was

The victorious Indian hockey team who trounced the host nation. (*Author's collection*)

sent home, asking for the services of A I S Dara, an Indian Army officer and one of the country's best hockey players (he would captain Pakistan in the 1948 London Olympics). But was he needed? By the time Dara joined the team, India had beaten Hungary 4–0, the USA 7–0 and Japan 9–0; Dara arrived in time for the semi-finals, a 10–0 massacre of France. As members of the British Empire, the Indians had been forced to march behind the Union Flag at the opening ceremony; in the dressing room before the final on 15 August, however, they reverently saluted the tricolour of the Indian National Congress which their assistant manager had taken with him to Berlin. Among the capacity crowd were the ruler of Baroda, the Princess of Bhopal and other prominent Indians who had travelled from other parts of Europe. They saw their team storm into a six-goal lead, by which time the Germans had begun to play rough. The home goalkeeper hit the Indian captain, Dhyan Chand, so hard in the mouth that the star man lost a tooth. Returning to the field after receiving treatment, the bare-footed Chand instructed his team to go easy on goals: 'We must teach them a lesson in ball control.' As the stunned crowd watched, the Indians repeatedly took the ball up to the German circle and then backpassed to dumbfound their opponents. The flood of goals eased off and the final score was 8–1 to India, who won its third successive Olympic hockey gold medal.

At a reception after the final, Hitler is alleged to have asked Chand – who had scored six goals – what his rank was in the Indian Army. When Chand replied that he was a *lancenaik* (lance-corporal), Hitler is said to have remarked: 'If you were a German, I would have made you at least a corporal.' (Some accounts make the unlikely claim that Hitler offered to make Chand a colonel if he emigrated to Germany.) In 1980, India issued a special postage stamp in Chand's honour.

On the May Field, more than 45,000 people watched Argentina beat Great Britain 11–0 in the final of the polo. Hungary and Germany, meanwhile, had been so outclassed that they were not included in the competition for gold and silver, instead playing off between themselves for the right to challenge the third team – Mexico – for the bronze medal. In the event, the Mexicans beat the Hungarians

Dhyan Chand, the Indian hockey captain, who reacted to some rough German tactics by telling his team to put on a display of ball control. (*Author's collection*)

16–2. The final placings were inevitable: Argentina boasted 130 polo clubs; Germany only one, the Hamburg club whose members played competitions among themselves. No more than five countries had ever competed in Olympic polo, which was discontinued after the Berlin Games.

Although football had been played at the Olympics since 1900, the official tournament dated back to the 1908 London Games when Great Britain defeated Denmark to claim the first soccer gold medal. Since that time soccer had been part of every Olympics, with the exception of the 1932 Games. The event had always been diluted by the fact that the world's best players were professionals and thus ineligible for the Olympics. Great Britain had not taken part in 1924 or 1928 after the home football associations withdrew from the game's ruling body, FIFA, over rows about payment of 'broken time' to amateurs; the British regarded the foreigners as 'shamateurs' anyway. But football was back for 1936, largely

Polo on the May Field between Argentina and Mexico. The Argentinians won this elimination match 15–5. (*Author's collection*)

because the organizers coveted the money generated by such a popular sport.

In Berlin, however, the tournament was marred by some ugly incidents. In one of the early games, between Italy and the USA, a German referee, Herr Weingartner, ordered off Achille Piccini of Italy, but he refused to leave the pitch. The full professional Italian team had won the World Cup in 1934, leaving Olympic representation to the Italian universities team, themselves regular winners of the World Student Games soccer title. The Italians, regarding themselves as giants of the game, were affronted by one of their players being dismissed against such an upstart soccer nation as America. Several Italians surrounded Weingartner, pinned his arms to his sides and covered his mouth with their hands. Remarkably, instead of a mass sending off, Piccini was allowed to remain on the pitch and Italy won 1–0.

That, however, was nothing compared to what happened five days later, when Austria and Peru met in the quarter-finals. Austria took a two-goal lead but Peru drew level with goals in the final fifteen minutes of normal time. The game had progressed to the second period of fifteen minutes' extra time when it too erupted into violence. There are conflicting versions, but what is certain is that there was a pitch invasion. Peruvian supporters rushed on to the field and, according to the Austrians, attacked one of their players. The Peruvian players took advantage of the uproar that followed, scoring two goals in quick succession to win 4–2. Austria appealed and an all-European jury ordered the game to be replayed with no spectators present. The entire Peruvian Olympic contingent promptly packed their suitcases and went home; the Colombians followed suit and also withdrew from the Games in support of their South American colleagues. In Lima, the German consulate was stoned and the Peruvian president, Oscar Benavides, was incandescent with rage over 'the crafty Berlin decision'. When it was pointed out that FIFA had made the ruling, not Germany, Benavides blamed the Communists instead.

Football was hugely popular in Germany, and the hosts desperately wanted to do well. They got off to an excellent start, beating Luxembourg 9–0 in the Post Stadium, then met Norway at the same venue. The large crowd included Hitler, Hess, Göring and

Austria attack the Peru goal during the football quarter-finals. The game ended in a riot and the entire Peruvian contingent went home. (*Author's collection*)

Goebbels, who wrote: 'The Führer is very excited, I can barely contain myself. A real bag of nerves.' But Norway scored after only six minutes, and then again six minutes from the end. Germany failed to find the net and Hitler, who had earlier planned to watch the rowing, left early in a huff. The British, meanwhile, laid themselves open to accusations that their preparations had been sloppy at best. This was the first time that the Olympic soccer team had been truly British – in past times it had really been an England amateur line-up – and they had received no coaching or fitness training; the players had simply met up ready to travel on the eve of the Games. According to the *Observer* in 2000, Daniel Petit, a member of the British team in 1936, had recently told a University College London academic, Rachel Cutler, that the letter he received from the FA about the Olympics dealt mostly with the uniform he would wear. There was a handwritten PS that said: 'As there is a month to go before we leave for Berlin, kindly take some exercise.' The obedient Petit promptly ran around his local park. It was no surprise, then, that Great Britain struggled to beat China 2–0 in the Mommsen Stadium, and then lost 5–4 to Poland in the Post Stadium. The British scored first but then went 5–1 down, a spirited fightback coming too late to save the day.

German flyweight boxer Willi Kaiser takes a breather before winning the gold medal by outpointing the Italian, Gavino Matta. (*Author's collection*)

It was Mussolini's student team which took the gold, beating Austria 2–1 in the final, watched by a crowd of 90,000. Italy's Annibale Frossi, who wore a headband and spectacles, scored the first goal of the game in the 70th minute, and although Karl Kainberger equalized on the stroke of full time, Frossi scored again in extra time. It was a hard-fought match, but considering what had gone on in the teams' earlier games, the Olympic football final was surprisingly free of controversy.

In the boxing, Jack Wilson, a bantamweight, became the tenth African-American to win a medal in the Games when he took silver after losing the decision to Ulderico Sergo of Italy. The Germans gained two golds: in the heavyweight division Herbert Runge outpointed the Argentinian, Guillermo Lovell;

Italian football supporters cheer on their team. (*Author's collection*)

The Italians threaten the Austrian defence in the football final. (*Author's collection*)

The Italian student football team which won the Olympic title. The bespectacled Annibale Frossi, scorer of both Italian goals, is third from the right. (*Author's collection*)

and at flyweight, Willi Kaiser was a points winner over the Italian, Gavino Matta. There was a double gold for France: Jean Despeaux (middleweight) and Roger Michelot (light-heavyweight).

On his way to the final, Michelot defeated a South African boxer called Robey Leibbrandt, a South African of German descent and an eccentric character who slept on bare boards and purged himself every two weeks by eating nothing but sand and charcoal for twenty-four hours. Considering his dedication, it is odd that Leibbrandt failed to appear for the bronze medal fight against Francisco Risiglione of Argentina. Injury was the official reason; unofficially it appeared that Leibbrandt had become distracted when sightseeing. He was perhaps fascinated by Nazi pomp. Back in South Africa, he joined the anti-British movement, Ossewa Brandwag. In 1937 he returned to Germany, learned to speak excellent German, grew a moustache like Hitler's, took the Nazi 'leadership-training' course and became a parachutist. In July 1941,

Looking slightly, self-conscious, Khadr el Touni of Egypt clutches his oak tree sapling after winning the middleweight weightlifting competition. Touni is flanked by two Germans: silver medallist Rudolf Ismayr (right) and Adolf Wagner, the bronze medal winner. (*Author's collection*)

a U-boat took Leibbrandt to a point off the desolate Namaqualand, South Africa. He set off on an orgy of sabotage, blowing up bridges and railway lines. Eventually captured, he was tried in Pretoria and condemned to death – greeting the judge's sentence with a cry of 'Heil Hitler!' – but this was later commuted to life imprisonment.

In the fencing, the Italians and Hungarians swept up the men's events, but in the only women's competition – the foil – all eyes were on the part-Jewish girl, Helene Meyer, who had returned from exile in America to represent Germany. There were several opinions about why she had agreed to wear the swastika on her fencing uniform: it would help her to full citizenship; she was desperate to see her ailing mother; that she wanted to strike a blow for Jewish athletes; it was simply for personal vanity and self-glory. Whatever her reason, Meyer won the silver medal, mounted the winners' podium, and gave the Nazi salute. The crowd roared their approval. Later in the day, Meyer shook hands with Hitler at an Olympic reception. She returned to America as a celebrity. Many people thought that she had been in a position to stand up to the

The part-Jewish fencer, Helene Meyer (extreme right), gives the Nazi salute after winning silver in the women's foil. (*Author's collection*)

Adolf Hitler chats to Hans von Tschammer und Osten aboard the yacht *Nixe* during the Olympic Regatta at Kiel. (*Author's collection*)

Nazis and should have done so. They felt she had shown Germany in a pleasant light, yet her paternal uncle was to perish in a concentration camp. The Helene Meyer story was one of the many contradictory episodes of the 1936 Olympic Games.

In the sailing events at Kiel, on the Baltic coast, Great Britain won gold in the International 6 m Class, while Italy, Germany and Holland shared the golds in the other three events. In the Monotype Class, 27-year-old Peter Scott, the only son of Antarctic explorer Captain Robert Falcon Scott, won bronze for Britain. In the 8 m Class, Jacob Tullin Thams of Norway won a silver medal, twelve years after he had won the ski jump at the first Olympic Winter Games.

There was gold for Britain in the rowing which was held on the Langer See at Grünau on Berlin's eastern edge. For the 2000 m course, new stands along the last 900 m could hold up to 20,000 spectators, and the banks were invariably packed as the rowers came home. They guaranteed the biggest crowds in the history of Olympic rowing. Britain's gold came in the double sculls when Jack Beresford and Leslie Southwood of Thames Rowing Club got home 6 seconds ahead of Germany's Willy Kaidel and Joachim Pirsch.

Yachting at Kiel on the Baltic coast. During the Olympic regatta, Keil harbour was full of German warships, while the Italian heavy cruiser *Gorizia* and the British light cruiser HMS *Neptune* also paid visits. Both ships were sunk by enemy action during the Second World War. (*Author's collection*)

Jack Beresford (left) and Leslie Southwood of Thames Rowing Club won gold for Britain in the double sculls, giving Beresford a remarkable Olympic record. (*Author's collection*)

The race was rowed in pouring rain – the weather had broken and that day more than half the rainfall normally expected for the whole month of August fell on Berlin – and gave Beresford a remarkable record. Now 37, he had won his first Olympic medal, a silver, back in 1920. The race was a thriller: the Germans looked certain of victory, but with 90 m to row, Beresford and Southwood drew level and went on to win by three lengths. Britain also won silver in the coxless fours, but overall it had been a disappointing return for her rowers who had been expected to do much better.

The 1936 Olympic Games were brought to a rousing climax when the best riders and horses of nineteen nations competed against each other in the show jumping section of the three-day event. The competition had begun with the dressage on the May Field, continued with the cross-country to the south of Döberitz (where, it was estimated, crowds of 50,000 turned out to watch) and the Olympic Village as well as on the steeplechase course at Ferbitz. It now concluded here in the Olympic Stadium. Since the modern Olympic Games had begun, no one country had ever before won all six gold medals in a sport. In 1936, however, Germany did just that in the equestrian competition. It was hardly surprising since they had been in full-time training for around eighteen months, while the British team, for instance, had been hastily assembled earlier in the year. The Germans – all army officers – excelled in everything they did, especially during the 37 km cross-country where there were several terrifying obstacles. For months the hosts had been practising daily on a replica course and they sailed around the real one, while foreign riders mostly got a ducking in the awkward water jump.

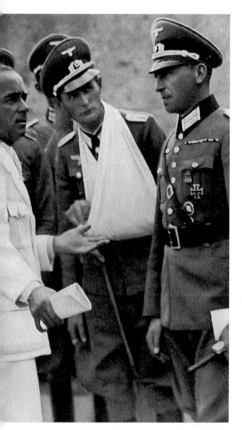

Lieutenant Freiherr von Wangenheim, with his arm in a sling, looks anxious. Despite a broken collar-bone he helped Germany to win the gold medal in the Prix des Nations equestrian event which closed the 1936 Olympic Games. (*Author's collection*)

It was reasonable to expect that on 16 August, the last day of the Games, the Olympic Stadium would be full for the Prix des Nations climax to the equestrian events; after all, it would be followed by the closing ceremony. But journalists

Young women of the Olympic Honorary Service. (*Author's collection*)

reported their amazement at the fact that by 10 a.m. more than 80,000 spectators were already in their seats. They were well rewarded. Although it seemed a foregone conclusion that Germany would complete a clean sweep of the gold medals, there was one act of drama to be played out. The previous day, Lieutenant Freiherr von Wangenheim had fallen from his mount, Kurfürst, during the steeplechase. The horse was unhurt but Wangenheim had suffered a broken collar-bone. Would he be able to ride again to give Germany a chance of the team event?

As each German horseman entered the arena, he saluted Hitler, who was in his place in the VIP box. But all eyes were on Wangenheim who stood at the entrance to the arena, his left arm in a sling. Finally, the sling was removed and Wangenheim's arm bound tightly to his side. Kurfürst, fresher and more enterprising than ever, went to work, clearing the first obstacles with tremendous leaps. At one of the next obstacles, a double jump, the horse was required to stop and turn between the first and second part of the obstacle. In his eagerness, Kurfürst rushed for the second part. He wanted to jump and Wangenheim was obliged to use force, pulling at the reins with both hands. Kurfürst yielded but rose vertically into the air, could not keep his balance on his hind legs, and fell backwards with his rider underneath him. Wangenheim quickly crawled out but his horse lay motionless. There was breathless silence. Then Kurfürst leapt to his feet as if he had reawakened. Wangenheim remounted him without help. From here to the end he made no further faults and Germany had also won the team competition. Even Chips Channon found it 'very exciting, even breathless', adding: 'Hitler ... seemed amiable and enjoying himself'.

By the time the last medals had been presented, twilight had given way to the blackness of night. It was time for the closing ceremony. For a moment, complete darkness lay over the stadium as Paul Winter's *Olympic Fanfare* rang out from the Marathon Tower, followed by Möllendorf's *Parade March* played by the Olympic Symphony Orchestra. Then

Searchlights pierce the sky as the Games are brought to a close. (*Author's collection*)

blue-white searchlight beams pierced the night, arcing to form a giant dome of light over the stadium. From the Marathon Gate, the flags of all the participating nations were moved forward to form up on both sides of the speakers' platform, facing the VIP box. Count Baillet-Latour stepped across the arena and mounted the platform to proclaim:

> In the name of the International Olympic Committee, after having offered to the Führer and Chancellor and to the German people, to the authorities of the town of Berlin and to the organizers of the Games, our deepest gratitude, we proclaim the closing of the eleventh Olympiad and, in accordance with tradition, we call upon the youth of every country to assemble in four years at Tokyo there to celebrate with us the Games of the twelfth Olympiad. May they display cheerfulness and concord so that the Olympic torch may be carried on with ever greater eagerness, courage and honour for the good of humanity throughout the ages. May it be so!

The Olympic Symphony Orchestra struck up and a 1,000-strong choir sang Beethoven's song of sacrifice *The Flaming Fire*. Meanwhile fifty-one white-uniformed girls of the Olympic Honorary Service stepped in front of the flags. The flags were lowered and the girls, who had previously handed the wreaths of victory to the winners, then fastened red-gold ribbons of remembrance on the flags, and attached wreaths on the points of the flagstaffs. It was, said the IOC official report, 'a beautiful scene, a truly solemn act'.

Then followed Major Feuchtinger's word of command: 'Haul down the flags!' Chorus and orchestra took up their music again, and from the May Field came the boom and flash of artillery cannons. Slowly, with a searchlight focused upon it, the Olympic flag was run down. German Olympic victors took the flag and slowly bore along the cinder track to the exit under the VIP box. On its bronze tripod the Olympic flame slowly expired to the solemn tolling of the great Olympic Bell.

A minute's silence was followed by a fanfare of bugles, and the Olympic flag was passed from William May Garland, president of the 1932 Los Angeles Games, via Baillet-Latour, to Julius Lippert, the State Commissioner of Berlin, for safekeeping until such time as it was needed again. Finally, the Olympic Symphony Orchestra struck up with Paul Hoffer's *Olympic Farewell*. As the flags of Germany, Greece and Japan were hoisted on the victory masts, the

The Olympic Stadium is set for the closing ceremony. (*Author's collection*)

The Olympic flag is borne away. (*Author's collection*)

words 'Berlin 1936, Athens 1896, Tokyo 1940' appeared on the giant announcement board.

Hitler had not spoken, but the crowd knew that he was there, somewhere in the dark. They roared his name and soon the stadium shook to one vast chorus of 'Heil Hitler!' and 'Sieg Heil!' They stood as one, right arms raised. Then came *Deutschland uber Alles* and the *Horst Wessel Lied*. The Berlin Olympic Games – some said the greatest of all Olympic Games – were at an end. Five weeks earlier, half an hour's drive to the north of the Olympic Stadium, a new concentration camp had been opened near the old Oranienburg camp. The first inmates of Sachsenhausen had been convicted of no crimes. Now the Olympics were over, would the world begin to take notice?

Chapter Fourteen

GHOSTS

In May 1946, Baldur von Schirach, the former head of the Hitler Youth, told his Nuremburg war crimes trial:

> Here is something I must tell you because I think I owe it to German youth. Hitler took very little interest in educational questions. As far as education was concerned, I received next to no suggestions from him. The only time when he did produce a real suggestion as far as athletic training was concerned was in 1935, I believe, when he told me that I should see to it that boxing should become more widespread among youth. I did so, but he never attended a youth boxing match. My friend von Tschammer und Osten, the Reich Sports Leader, and I tried very often to make him go to other sporting events, particularly to skiing contests and ice hockey championships in Garmisch, but apart from the Olympic Games, it was impossible to get him to attend.

Ironically, for a man who was not remotely interested in sport, the German Führer was to witness some extraordinary examples of athletic prowess at the Berlin Olympics. Many people thought that the very peak of human physical achievement in track and field had been reached at the 1932 Los Angeles Games. Yet four years later, seventeen Olympic and five world records were broken in the men's events and five Olympic records fell in the women's. Jesse Owens alone passed previous Olympic records on no less than eleven occasions. It was Germany, however, who emerged at the top of the medals table – there was no official table but the Germans invented a fair scoring system – with thirty-three gold, twenty-six silver and thirty bronze. The United States collected twenty-four gold, twenty silver and twelve bronze. By comparison, the rest – Britain had four gold – were nowhere.

Germany did not only wallow in medal glory, however. Everyone agreed that the organization in Berlin had been second to none, the pomp and pageantry something to remember for the rest of their lives, the entertainment breathtaking, the food and wine – especially at the dozens of official functions – as good as could be found anywhere in the world, and the German people themselves polite and friendly. There was a smattering of petty crime, but no instances of any Jew, or other non-Aryan, suffering verbal abuse or worse. Despite the overbearing militaristic nature of the Olympic festival, most visitors left Berlin with an impression that here was a nation working hard to re-establish its economy and its place at the international table, a nation which apparently liked to play hard too. There were some mixed reactions, of course – Chips Channon wrote: 'Berlin, of all the cities I have ever know, next perhaps to New York in boom days, has the most stimmung [mood or atmosphere] and the least beauty.' – but overall, no one could argue, it seemed, that the Nazis had delivered a splendid Olympiad.

But at what cost? In November 1935, George Messersmith, by then the American ambassador in Vienna, had written to Cordell Hull, the Secretary of State, telling him that there were many 'wise and well-informed' observers in Europe who believed that the staging, or otherwise, of the Olympics in Berlin would play an important role in determining the future of Europe. The importance of the Olympic Games, he told his boss, could not be exaggerated. The following year, Messersmith went even further:

> To the [Nazi] Party and to the youth of Germany, the holding of the Olympic Games in Berlin in 1936 has become the symbol of the conquest of the world by National Socialist doctrine. Should the Games not be held in Berlin, it would be one of the most serious blows which National Socialist prestige could suffer.

It is a matter of historical record, of course, that the American administration chose not only to ignore the implications of the Berlin Olympics but also the very threat of Hitler and Nazism itself.

Whatever America's reaction, however, it is impossible to judge what effect the IOC's moving the Games from Germany to a more acceptable country would have had. Indeed, that was surely an impossibility anyway. Barcelona, the runner-up to Berlin, was just about to become embroiled in a bloody civil war; and it would have taken a huge logistical effort for any other city to stage the Olympics. Had it been a viable option, as Messersmith pointed out, then Nazi prestige would have been badly damaged. But surely that would not have stopped Hitler? Domestically, the Games were a great success for the Führer. But if Germany had been robbed of them, then far from damaging Hitler in the eyes of his own people, it may well have served to accelerate his progress; the Nazi machine was already gaining impressive momentum. After a 1935 plebiscite, the Saar Territory – the administration of which the League of Nations had assigned to France after the First World War – had become a German province, albeit peacefully and democratically. But between the Winter and Summer Games, the Rhineland had been illegally reoccupied without opposition. Germany was rearming at such an alarming rate that Britain and France were about to lose their opportunity to stop Hitler by force. Had Germany lost the Olympic Games – or even if just the United States had boycotted them – it is most likely that Hitler would have blamed the Jews and the Bolsheviks, and then got on with persecuting those within Germany while at the same time putting more detail to his plans for the Thousand-Year Reich and world domination.

Perhaps with the benefit of hindsight some, like Lord Killanin, IOC president 1972–80, felt that holding the Games in Berlin actually drew attention to the evils of Nazism. Writing in 1983, Killanin, who was a young newspaper reporter based in London in 1936, said:

> To claim that the Games in 1936 made the situation in Germany worse is wrong. Rather the opposite, for the fact that the Games were in Germany drew the world's attention to events … For everyone who might shut his eyes to what was going on, another would be disturbed and at least talk about the situation when he got home.

Apart from noticing that there were soldiers and military bands everywhere, it is hard to imagine what else foreign visitors saw that would have alarmed them. All anti-Jewish posters had been removed and the newly opened Sachsenhausen concentration camp just up the road was hardly on the Berlin tourist department's list of places to visit.

The reality was more effectively summed by the American journalist William Shirer, who on 16 August, the day of the closing ceremony, wrote in his diary:

> I'm afraid the Nazis have succeeded with their propaganda. First, the Nazis have run the Games on a lavish scale never before experienced, and this has appealed to the athletes. Second, the Nazis have put up a very good front for the general visitors, especially the big businessmen.

In 1984, Shirer concluded: 'Hitler, we who covered the Games had to concede, turned the Olympics into a dazzling propaganda success for his barbarian regime.'

Whatever the outcome of a boycott or total withdrawal might have been, why was Nazi Germany allowed to stage the Olympic Games? Members of the IOC were certainly not bribed, over and above being subjected to the usual wining and dining that goes with any Olympic bid. But they were acutely aware of the financial implications to their organization, and to sports bodies around the world, if the Games had been cancelled. And there were no national governments trying to stop Hitler in 1935 or 1936, or even encouraging a boycott of the Games. So providing the rules of sport had not been broken, was it up to the IOC to make such a monumental decision? The Nazis could not object to Jewish or black athletes from other nations; and until the eleventh hour they had at least one Jew – Gretel Bergmann – lined up for their own team. On the face of it, the IOC's position was a difficult one. What can be said with certainty is that, just as the Nazis benefited from a huge propaganda coup, so the 1936 Games were given a higher profile than any other Olympics before them. The absolute standard was also set: politics and sport cannot be kept apart; and any nation, no matter what its political regime, can stage the Olympic Games even if – as in the cases of Moscow in 1980 and Los Angeles in 1984 – major nations boycott them.

So the bigger question is not why were the Olympics held in Berlin, but why were Hitler's territorial ambitions allowed to proceed unchallenged until war was inevitable? It is difficult to hold the International Olympic Committee even the tiniest bit responsible for that.

They were also operating in different times. On 14 August – as the IOC and Organizing Committee enjoyed a luncheon party before going by steamer to Grünau to witness the final regatta events – there was great excitement in America's Deep South where the great Olympian, Jesse Owens, had been born. In the town of Owensboro, Kentucky, 15,000 men, women and children held all-night parties as they waited for the public hanging of a 26-year-old black man called Rainey Bethea who had been convicted of the rape and murder of a 70-year-old white widow, Lischia Edwards. New shrubs and flowers had been planted in the yard of the Daviess County Courthouse, and Sheriff Florence Thompson became concerned that, as they watched the execution, such a crowd of people might trample the blooms she had just planted. The media frenzy ensured that this would be America's last public execution, but it serves to illustrate that, at the beginning of the twenty-first century, it is perhaps unwise to judge world reaction to events that happened in Germany in the middle of the twentieth.

In London, meanwhile, the Canadian team was having trouble at its hotel where some guests complained about having to share the facilities with two black men, Phil Edwards, the team captain, and Sam Richardson, a triple-jumper. Ab Conway, an 800 m runner, recalled:

> The officials, with full team backing, decided not to stay at that hotel as a team. I think probably the best quote came from Cathleen Hughes-Hallett, a girl fencer. When this little episode happened at the hotel she said: 'If this hotel is too good for Phil Edwards, it's too good for me.'

Again, while one can in no way draw a parallel between events in Nazi Germany and the colour prejudice of a few well-heeled Londoners, one has to acknowledge that in the 1930s, racism was everywhere, and quite the norm.

Berlin's Olympic Stadium pictured in the late summer of 1945, after the war in Europe had come to an end. (*Melvin C. Shaffer Collection*)

In Germany, the suspension of the anti-Jewish campaign was brief. William E. Dodd, the US ambassador, reported that Jews awaited 'with fear and trembling' the end of the Olympic truce. Two days after the Games, Captain Wolfgang Fürstner, the former head of the Olympic Village, committed suicide after he was dismissed from active military service because of his Jewish ancestry. Fürstner it was who in 1934 had suggested the formation of the Olympic Honorary Youth Service to assist athletes, the Organizing Committee, the technical department, the directors at competition venues and the administrative headquarters at the Olympic Village. Fürstner, former head of the Wehrmacht's sporting programme, had done an excellent job in building and organizing the Village run by the Germany Army. But a few weeks before the Games he was quietly moved aside, to be replaced by Lieutenant Colonel Werner von und zu Gilsa, with Fürstner now nominally his assistant. A few days after the Games ended, and after attending a banquet given in von und zu Gilsa's honour, Fürstner returned to his barracks and shot himself; he realized that he had no future under the Nazis. The official version of his death was that he had been killed in a car crash, but the truth soon leaked out to foreign journalists, which meant that Fürstner was at least given a full military funeral, although the now deserted Olympic Village was the site of some obscene graffiti about 'the Jew Fürstner'.

In the two months that followed the Games, Nazi persecution of the Jews resumed as further laws were aimed at them. The Berlin Labour Court ruled that German employees who married Jews or other non-Aryans could be dismissed from their jobs, while Jewish-owned employment agencies were closed, as was the Association of Independent Artisans of the Jewish Faith, a German Jewish mutual aid society. Hans Frank, Reich Minister without Portfolio, explained the need to exclude Jews from the legal profession:

We National Socialists have started with anti-Semitism in our fight to free the German people, to re-establish a German Reich … It took all the self-confidence of German manhood to withstand and to triumph in this fight to substitute the German spirit for Jewish corruption.

The Reich Chamber of Culture ordered all Jewish art dealers in Berlin to close their galleries by the end of the year. Jewish teachers were forbidden to tutor Aryan children. Jews who converted to Christianity and were baptized were still declared Jewish. In July,

Victor Klemperer had wondered if, once the Games were over, it would be open season on Jews again. Now he had the answer. In late August, Klemperer was to write: 'I often very much doubt whether we shall actually survive the Third Reich.'

Only eight days after the closing ceremony, the world had a further indication of Hitler's plans when two-year mandatory military service becomes compulsory in Germany. On the same day, 24 August, Mussolini broadcast on Italian radio: 'We can, at any time, in a few hours, mobilise eight million men ... The armaments race cannot be checked. We do not believe in the absurdity of perpetual peace.' Earlier, while being annoyed at Italy's overall performance at the Olympics, the Italian dictator had awarded £80 to each of his country's eight gold medallists, and smaller amounts to the fourteen Italian winners of silver and bronze. Hitler, who in November 1936 signed the anti-Comintern pact with Japan which declared the two nations' hostility towards international Communism, spent the next twelve months wooing Mussolini. Then, in 1939, Hitler invaded Poland and the world war that had been inevitable for several months was finally ignited. There would be no Olympic Games in Tokyo in 1940; nor in London in 1944 for that matter.

The fates of the Nazi hierarchy, either by their own hand or by that of their executioner, are well documented. For the key figures in the 1936 Berlin Olympic Games, there were to be differing fates. Carl Diem, the man credited with inventing the modern Olympic torch run, remained one of the most creative – and eventually controversial – figures in the history of German sport. From 1938 until 1945 he was director of the International Olympic Institute in Berlin. Just as he had worked with the National Socialist regime, so, after the Second World War, Diem was to cooperate with successive West German governments. From 1945 to 1947 he was director of the Institute of Physical Education and School Hygiene at the University of Berlin; then co-founder and, until his death at the age of 80 in 1962, chancellor of the Sport University in Cologne. He advised several other governments around the world on sports issues and his full list of appointments and remarkable achievements and honours is far too long to recount here. Suffice to say that for half a century from 1912, Diem was involved in most of the major decisions in German sport.

Yet in the 1990s a debate raged over whether the German streets named after him – something like a hundred throughout the country – should be renamed. There were those who felt that Diem himself was a National Socialist, or at the very least an apologist for the regime. His more vehement critics pointed out that at the Reichs Sports Field on 18 March 1945, as Russian troops neared Berlin, Diem had addressed soldiers of the *Volkssturm* (People's Storm) and new recruits of the Hitler Youth. The People's Storm militia effectively conscripted all males between the ages of 16 and 60 who did not already serve in a military unit; it was a last, desperate attempt by Hitler as the Allies closed in. There were claims that Diem had exhorted young Germans, some barely out of school, to fight to the death for the Third Reich; it seems more likely that he was simply ordered to give a general rallying call. Diem could perhaps better be viewed as an opportunist, not so much on a personal level but in the interests of the causes in which he believed. His aim was always to develop German sports, so he worked with whichever government was in power. True, under the Nazis this meant standing by as Jews and other non-Ayran sportsmen and women were persecuted; but just before Hitler came to power in 1933, Diem had been described mockingly in the National Socialist press as a 'white Jew'; and he had employed Jews in the work of the Organizing Committee. His biggest mistake may simply have been in believing that he could serve sport and not be unduly troubled by the Nazis.

The half-Jewish Theodor Lewald, meanwhile, enjoyed no such career under National Socialism following the Berlin Olympics. Already removed as president of the German Olympic Committee in 1934, in 1938 he was also forced to resign from the IOC; he was, of course, twenty-two years older than Diem. Lewald died in Berlin in April 1947, aged 86.

By the end of the 1930s, Hans von Tschammer und Osten, who as Reich Sports Leader had been responsible for carrying out Nazi policy of racial and religious segregation in German sport – and for helping to camouflage it for a few weeks in 1936 – had lost much of his influence. In March 1937, perhaps in an attempt to re-establish his credentials, he had called for all youth sports organizations to affiliate to the Hitler Youth. Eighteen months later his department had been renamed the National Socialist Department of Physical Education. Von Tschammer und Osten died in March 1943, from pneumonia. Baldur von Schirach told his Nuremburg trial that von Tschammer und Osten had a brother who had served as an officer in the Wehrmacht. In January 1946, a Major General von Tschammer und Osten (also named as Hans in some accounts) was sentenced to death by a USSR tribunal at Kiev for atrocities committed in the Ukraine; he was hanged the same day.

Karl Ritter van Halt, the president of the 1936 Winter Games, continued in banking until the end of the Second World War, and also carried on his sporting duties. Despite the war, he somehow managed to become president of the European Commission of the IAAF from 1942 to 1945. In the latter year he was imprisoned by the Russians and spent five years in a Soviet camp while remaining a nominal member of the IOC. When the Federal Republic of Germany's Olympic Committee was constituted in September 1949, its first president was the Duke of Mecklenburg-Schwerin, who had served with Ritter van Halt on the IOC back in the 1930s. Ritter van Halt took over the German OC presidency from 1951 to 1961. He remained an IOC member until his death in Munich in 1964.

When Jesse Owens returned to America in August 1936, it was not to lucrative advertising and product endorsement campaigns. Despite his Olympic triumphs, the financial instability of the Owens family continued. In an effort to provide for them, he left college before his senior year to run professionally. For a while he was a runner-for-hire, pitting himself against anything from people to motorcycles. He raced against some of Major League Baseball's fastest ballplayers, always giving them a 10 yds start before easily beating them. The Negro Baseball League even hired him to race against thoroughbred horses before games. It was almost a freak show.

But then he was given the opportunity to demonstrate another side of himself, taking on public-speaking engagements. Owens proved an articulate and entertaining lecturer. He started his own public relations firm and travelled around America, speaking on behalf of companies like Ford and the United States Olympic Committee. Owens stressed the importance of religion, hard work and loyalty. He also sponsored and participated in many youth sports programmes in underprivileged neighbourhoods. In 1976, Owens was awarded the highest honour a civilian of the United States can receive: President Gerald Ford awarded him the Medal of Freedom. On 31 March 1980, at the age of 66, Jesse Owens died in Tuscon, Arizona, from lung cancer. Ironically, the greatest Olympian of all had, for years, been a heavy smoker. Today, one of the main thoroughfares leading to the Olympic Stadium in Berlin is named Jesse Owens Allee.

The stadium itself, centrepiece of Hitler's Reich Sports Field upon which the gaze of the sporting world had rested for those two weeks in August 1936, was one of the few buildings in Berlin to survive the Second World War almost unscathed. Despite heavy Allied bombing of the Reich capital, and the battle around the

The Olympic Swimming Stadium was used almost immediately after the German surrender by the occupying military and their guests. (*Melvin C. Shaffer Collection*)

stadium in April 1945 as the Russian Army fought to capture it, only the Olympic Bell and Bell Tower met an undignified end. In 1945, the tower caught fire and the fierce heat conducted up, as though through a chimney, caused the steel framework to buckle. Two years later, the tower was demolished by British military engineers. The Olympic Bell, cracked by the blast, was buried nearby, to be dug up in December 1956 and placed on a platform near the south gate of the Olympic Stadium. The name of the soldier who decided to test his prowess by shooting at the defenceless bell with an anti-tank gun will never be known, but in the early 1960s, the Bell Tower was rebuilt according to Werner March's original plan. Today, the Olympic Stadium in Berlin, with all its seats now under cover, has changed dramatically. Yet it is still recognizable in its Reich Sports Field setting; the view from the new bell tower is much the same, looking over the May Field to the Marathon Arch and into the stadium itself which is again one of Germany's great sporting venues. It is impossible to visit and not to feel the ghosts of 1936.

PRINCIPAL SOURCES

Books

Arnaud, P and Riordan, J (eds), *Sport and International Politics 1900–1941*, London, Spon, 1998

Bachrach, Susan D, *The Nazi Olympics*, Boston and New York, Little, Brown & Co., 2000

Channon, Sir Henry, *Chips: The Diaries of Sir Henry Channon*, ed. Robert Rhodes James, London, Weidenfeld, 1993

Cohen, Stan, *The Games of '36*, Missoula, Mont., Pictorial Histories Publishing Co. 1996

Glickman, Marty and Isaacs, Stan, *The Fastest Kid on the Block: The Marty Glickman Story*, Syracuse, NY, Syracuse University Press, 1996

Hart-Davies, Duff, *Hitler's Games*, London, Century Hutchinson, 1986

Harvey, Charles (ed.) *Encyclopaedia of Sport*, London, Sampson, Low, Marston & Co., 1959

Henry, Bill, *An Approved History of the Olympic Games*, New York, G P Putnam's Sons, 1948

Hesse-Lichtenberger, Ulrich, *Tor! The Story of German Football*, London, WSC Books, 2002

Hitler, Adolf, *Mein Kampf* (English edn), London, Hurst & Blackett, 1933

Inglis, Simon, *The Football Grounds of Europe*, London, Willow Books, 1990

Iremonger, F A, *William Temple, Archbishop of Canterbury: His Life and Letters*, Oxford, Oxford University Press, 1948

Killanin, Lord, *My Olympic Years*, London, Martin, Secker & Warburg, 1983

Klemperer, Victor, *I Shall Bear Witness: The Diaries of Victor Klemperer 1933-41*, London, Weidenfeld & Nicolson, 1998

Krüger, Arnd and Murray, William (eds), *The Nazi Olympics: Sport, Politics and Appeasement in the 1930s*, Chicago, University of Illinois Press, 2003

Lovesey, Peter, *The Official Centenary History of the Amateur Athletic Association*, London, Guinness Superlatives, 1979

Lunn, Sir Arnold, *The Kandahar Story*, London, Allen & Unwin, 1969

McRae, Donald, *In Black and White*, London, Scribner, 2002

Martin, Simon, *Football and Fascism: The National Game under Mussolini*, Oxford, Berg, 2004.

Miller, David, *Stanley Matthews: The Authorized Biography*, London, Pavilion Books, 1989

Morse, Arthur D, *While Six Million Died: A Chronicle of American Apathy*, New York, Overlook Press, 1998

Rampersad, Arnold, *Jackie Robinson: A Biography*, New York, Ballantine Publishing Group, 1998

Richter, Frederich (ed.), *The XIth Olympic Games, Berlin, 1936, Official Report*, vols 1 and 2, Berlin, Wilhelm Limpert, 1937

Riordan, J W and Kruger, A, *The International Politics of Sport in the 20th Century*, London: Spon, 1999

Shirer, William, *The Rise and Fall of the Third Reich*, New York, Touchstone, 1981

Shirer, William, *The Nightmare Years, 1930–1940*, New York, Bantam, 1985

Shirer, William, *Berlin Diary: The Journal of a Foreign Correspondent 1934–1941*, Baltimore, Johns Hopkins University Press, 2002

Snyder, Louis L, *Encyclopedia of the Third Reich*, New York, Paragon House, 1989

Wallechinsky, David, *The Complete Book of the Olympics*, London, Aurum Press, 2000

Other publications

Daily Express

Daily Mail

Die Woche, Olympia 1936, published in Germany, 1936

Germany: The Olympic Year 1936, Berlin, Volk & Reich Verlag, 1936

International Journal for the History of Sport

Journal of Sport History

Manchester Guardian

New York Times

Observer

Official Bulletin of the International Olympic Committee (English editions), 1932, 1933, 1934, 1935, 1936

Olympic Games 1936 (official magazine published in monthly issues 1935–6)

Riefenstahl, Leni (dir.), *Olympia: Part 1, Fest der Völker; Part 2, Fest der Schönheit* (film)

The Times

INDEX